MW00805451

Published by Rowman & Littlefield
A wholly owned subsidiary of The Rowman & Littlefield Publishing Group, Inc.
4501 Forbes Boulevard, Suite 200, Lanham, Maryland 20706
www.rowman.com

Unit A, Whitacre Mews, 26-34 Stannary Street, London SE11 4AB

Original illustrations created by Lisa Malveaux.

British Library Cataloguing in Publication Information Available

Library of Congress Cataloging-in-Publication Data Available

ISBN 978-1-4758-2864-1 (cloth : alk. paper)
ISBN 978-1-4758-2865-8 (pbk. : alk. paper)

♾™ The paper used in this publication meets the minimum requirements of American National Standard for Information Sciences—Permanence of Paper for Printed Library Materials, ANSI/NISO Z39.48-1992.

Printed in the United States of America

Unexpected Influence

Women Who Helped
Shape the Early
Community College Movement

Anne-Marie McCartan

AMERICAN
ASSOCIATION OF
COMMUNITY
COLLEGES

ROWMAN & LITTLEFIELD
Lanham • Boulder • New York • London

who understood why I was at the office so many weekends over the course of the three years it took to research and write this book.

For lack of a publisher, the manuscript for this book languished after its completion in 2005. In 2015, I approached Walter G. Bumphus, who was at the helm of the AACC. As a self-acknowledged history buff, he understood that that organization had a responsibility to help get the stories of these women published. For his support I am genuinely grateful.

Finally, I am deeply indebted to the women who are the subjects of this book. Those I had the privilege to interview in person were remarkably forthcoming, believing, I trust, that allowing others to gain insights into the development of community colleges was important enough to share with me their life story.

Acknowledgments

During the busiest year of this project, I was provost and dean of faculty at Richard Bland College of the College of William and Mary. Then-president James B. McNeer graciously supported my research. A dear friend provided travel funds so that I could interview those subjects still living. The miracles of modern connectivity allowed me to track down and make contact with a group of men and women who were influential figures during those years. I especially wish to acknowledge Edmund J. Gleazer, Jr., Rod Risley, John Roueche, Paul Elsner, Alfredo de los Santos, and Wayne Stein, who gave generously of their time and granted lengthy, insightful interviews. Marjane Ambler, then editor of the *Tribal College Journal*, was invaluable in assisting me with the chapter on women of the tribal colleges.

Collectively, I offer thanks to the dozens of people listed under "Interviews with the Author" for their willingness to share their recollections and opinions about this important historical period and the women who helped shape it. In speaking with the subjects of this book and with those who knew them, I kept realizing the rich history that would be lost if these stories were not put into print. As the records on individual leaders from this era are largely fragmented or nonexistent, it is through collecting oral accounts that some important history can be reconstructed.

Additionally, thanks are due to Judy Blevins and Kristin Thrower at Richard Bland College; the library staff at Los Angeles Pierce and Los Angeles City Colleges; Carrole Wolin of the National Institute for Leadership Development; Jan Grizel, Kristina Lopez, and Ninfa Trejo at Pima Community College; and Martha Parham at the American Association of Community Colleges (AACC). Special thanks to John, Joseph, and Mario Accordino,

Contents

Unexpected Influence

Preface

The genesis of this work is personal. As a young woman beginning my career in higher education, I sought out learning opportunities to expand my exposure to people and ideas outside my graduate student experience. A succession of varied and engaging professional assignments put me in proximity to a series of mentors, a number of whom were prominent leaders in American higher education. Those mentors who were female inspired me deeply, not only because they served as role models for professional achievement but because they interacted with me as a peer—an honor for which I wanted to feel worthy.

Beyond personal gratitude for having known and learned from these (and other) women, I began to comprehend their larger contributions to higher education and, in particular, to America's community colleges. Contemporaneously, I was amassing a personal collection of biographies and autobiographies of women from this country and abroad, famous and not so famous, historical and contemporary. Having read more than one hundred such accounts, I became increasingly intrigued with the absorbing stories of these women's lives and the scant recognition of their contributions.

So why not combine my good fortune of having access to a group of women who contributed greatly to my own field with my extensive exposure to lives of interesting women as told through their biographies? Thus began a journey spanning three years (2003–2005), searching for subjects for this book, interviewing them and other key informants, and writing.

I began the project by researching the literature on junior colleges prior to World War II. Anyone who has studied America's community colleges knows well the names associated with this period—William Rainey

Harper, Leonard V. Koos, Walter Eells, and B. Lamar Johnson. As the potential for junior college education began to be realized after the war, the influence of others was felt, notably Jesse P. Bogue, Leland Medsker, James Wattenbarger, and S. V. Martorana.

During the years of growth and expansion, figures such as Edmund J. Gleazer, Jr., B. Lamar Johnson, Terry O'Banion, Dale Parnell, and William H. Meardy were prominent nationally. Prolific university researchers, including Richard L. Alfred, George A. Baker III, Arthur M. Cohen, Richard C. Richardson Jr., John E. Roueche, and Dale Tillery, published extensively and educated the next generation of community college leaders during the seventies and eighties. And highly visible presidents such as Joseph Cosand, Paul A. Elsner, Joseph Fordyce, Peter Masiko, Robert H. McCabe, Donald G. Phelps, Bill J. Priest, Abel Sykes, George B. Vaughan, and Norman Watson were active in national leadership positions or in publicizing the accomplishments of their colleges and inspiring others to take notice.

Examining the contributions of these prominent men shows that many achieved influence through their national leadership roles or by writing books on the evolving junior and community college movement.[1]

It also reveals a glaring, salient omission of women's names. Did any females make unique contributions that affected the direction, image, goals, or curriculum of the movement? Delving into this question through extensive interviews and further reading reassured me that, indeed, a number of women made singular contributions to the community college movement.

Introduction

This book is organized into three parts. The first sets the stage by providing historical context of the place of women in junior and community colleges during the period covered, roughly from the issuance of the President's [Truman] Commission Report on Higher Education in 1947 through 1990.

The second part highlights—through twelve in-depth profiles—the women I chose to feature. Their profiles are sequenced in relation to the time that they were most visible on the national scene. It was challenging to decide how to profile each of these remarkable women. In "Appendix A: Methodology," I describe the selection process and list those I selected to profile.

In conducting the research and writing the profiles, I often felt as Carolyn Heilburn describes, that "biographers of women have had not only to choose one interpretation over another but, far more difficult, actually to reinvent the lives their subjects led, discovering from what evidence they could find the processes and decisions, the choices and unique pain, that lay beyond the life stories of these women."[1]

Ultimately, I strove to communicate three things in the telling of each story. First, I wanted to provide a personal and professional chronology. Some of these women were daughters of college-educated fathers and mothers; most were not. Some were on a college trajectory early on; others never imagined continuing their educations after high school. Some married and had children; others did not. I include these details because I wanted to approach each subject as a whole person, believing that her contributions were influenced by the combination of natural talents and abilities, and by those who parented them, reared them, taught them, mentored them, or even treated them unfairly along the way.

I was able to locate photographs of the women from the period during which they made their contributions. Lisa Malveaux (www.studio malveaux.com) brought the photographs to life through her remarkable illustration skills.

Second, it seemed important to document how each woman found herself associated with the community college movement; certainly in this era, community colleges had yet to attain general respectability or even understanding, and career paths for women in higher education were often limited.

And finally, the profiles detail the professional situations of these women in order to document this period of history in community colleges and to understand how women fared within this context. For all of the importance and growing influence of community colleges during this period, few books document the people—women *or* men—who built this remarkable new educational institution.[2]

The book's third part, "Reflections," examines the picture that arises from researching the lives and contributions of these women. What lessons can women—and men—take away from their stories? How are community colleges different because of their contributions? Overarching issues such as racial and gender discrimination, the importance of mentors, the role of federal and foundation funding, balancing personal and professional lives, and motivating factors are considered.

The book's title, *Unexpected Influence*, emphasizes the notion that all of these women attained prominence by happenstance rather than by virtue of a carefully planned career trajectory. Driven by an idea, a passion, or a talent, they made significant contributions: to high-achieving students seeking to develop their potential, to women wanting to move into leadership positions, to counselors making the transition to dynamic student-development professionals, to faculty seeking to enhance their teaching skills, and to populations underserved by the existing educational system.

In writing these profiles, my own sense of appreciation for all of the pioneers of this movement was enhanced. My hope for readers is that this book shines a spotlight on the contributions of an extraordinary group of women. Truly, they deserve a prominent place in the pages of the history of America's community college movement.

Part I

SETTING THE STAGE

- A doctoral student decides to use her experience as a former nurse to design a curriculum to train nurses in two years—in an educational setting rather than a hospital setting, which was the norm in the 1940s. The national community college association, searching to expand the scope of junior college education beyond pre-transfer course, provides backing to her to take this idea nationally. By the time the pilot project is completed in 1956, forty two-year colleges have started preparing students for careers in nursing.
- By the early 1960s, those in community colleges were convinced that two-year colleges should be taken seriously as a path to the baccalaureate for nontraditional students. Yet, armed with little other than anecdotal evidence to back their claims, they were finding few believers outside their circle. But when two researchers at a higher-education think tank at the University of California, Berkeley, published a study tracking seven thousand students transferring from two- to four-year colleges, their assertions were validated. The study found that 62 percent achieved the baccalaureate degree within three years after transferring. For the next four decades, the research produced by the female author of this study continued to be among the most respected quantitative look at student behavior in community colleges.
- As community colleges grew in number, they began to find that the demand for their services was outpacing the depth of experience they had to meet these needs. But the woman heading the newly created community college unit in the U.S. Department of Education in 1972 had an idea: she would convince her superiors that community colleges were eligible for funding under an existing federal grant program then serv-

ing another sector of higher education. Over the course of seven years, 150 rural community colleges benefited from a nationwide consortium aimed at developing their capacities in curriculum, community services, fund-raising, and student development.

- In the early years, community colleges worked hard at separating themselves from their historical connection to secondary education. One woman involved in helping create a new community college in the early 1970s thought just the opposite: the promise that community colleges were realizing with nontraditional adult students might be just what was needed for capable but high-risk high school students. So she went about systematically removing the political and financial barriers to found a high school within a community college. The phenomenal success of those students who were thought unlikely to complete high school caught the attention of colleges and has been replicated in various forms around the country.

- Despite the huge number of women working in all capacities in community colleges in the 1980s, only twenty-one out of some one thousand presidents were female. Two women with distinctly different backgrounds and personalities paired up to create and run a leadership development program to help women move up the ranks to the presidency. Believing that women needed separate training, strategies, and assistance to counteract insidious gender discrimination, these women crisscrossed the country for eight years offering workshops to thousands of promising women leaders in community colleges.

These are just five stories that remain previously unrecorded about a group of women who made singular contributions during the years of the phenomenal growth of America's two-year colleges. Determined to document their contributions and those of several other influential females, I set about identifying, interviewing, and writing the personal and professional stories of sixteen such leaders (see "Appendix A: Methodology").

These sixteen women—whose stories appear as twelve mini-biographies or "profiles" in part II (in roughly chronological order)—rose to prominence in a time when gender barriers existed, when little was expected of them professionally, and when choosing community college education as the focus of their work meant going against the established academic grain. The stories of these women, taken together, amplify the history of community colleges during this period. In the course of their lives, these women made their mark on the evolving—and, at the time, unique—educational innovation known as the community college.

Before proceeding to the individual profiles, a brief history is in order. It is neither necessary nor feasible to review in-depth the history of the junior and community college movement for this book.[1] Rather, three developments are important in placing the contributions of these women in historical context: the evolution and growth of community colleges, the changing social context for women, and the extension of universal access to groups previously underserved by higher education.

FOUNDING OF THE MOVEMENT AND ITS GROWTH

The roots of the modern-day community college generally are traced to William Rainey Harper's separation of the first two years of study at the University of Chicago into lower-division "Academic Colleges" and upper-division "University" or "Senior Colleges" in the early 1890s. Similar innovations began taking place elsewhere in Illinois, Michigan, Indiana, and other midwestern states. Private and religious-affiliated colleges constituted the majority of early junior colleges.

Fueled by the lack of higher education availability to the widespread growing population in California and a belief by universities that lower-division study was essentially an extension of high school, that state was ripe for expansion of the junior college movement by the turn of the century. Its most prominent proponents were David Starr Jordan, president of Stanford University, and Alexis Lange, a faculty member at the University of California.

Additionally, in 1907, a state law authorized school districts to offer post–high school courses, which led to the establishment of dozens of public junior colleges, mostly in small communities. Although these lower-division colleges or extensions of high school emphasized general academics, many emphasized career development, particularly for students intending to enter teaching, business, the industrial arts, and agriculture.

An organization to better define and promote junior colleges was founded at the first national meeting of two-year college leaders in St. Louis in 1920.

Although junior colleges numbered some two hundred by that time, only thirty-four delegates attended, largely members from private, religious-oriented colleges.

Those who were gathered elected officers and named the new organization the American Association of Junior Colleges (AAJC). By the end of the decade, membership had grown to 210 active colleges and 15 associate members. The number of public colleges continued to grow, reaching 146 in 1927, with most of the expansion occurring in California, Iowa, and Texas.[2]

Student enrollment continued to build during the Great Depression, particularly due to the fact that President Franklin D. Roosevelt's Federal Emergency Relief Administration channeled funds to communities to establish "emergency junior colleges."[3] Enrollment in public junior colleges began to far outpace growth in their private and religious-affiliated counterparts. All types of two-year colleges numbered about 520 by 1936.[4] Although the term "community college" cannot be traced to a single first source, it began to be used in general terms by this time.

In 1938, the AAJC elected its first female president, Katherine Denworth of Bradford College, a private junior college in Massachusetts. (It would be another thirteen years before another woman was elected to that post by her peers.) To support the need for full-time professional staff and a permanent headquarters for the organization, at the 1939 convention, AAJC membership approved a reorganization plan to pay its executive secretary, Walter Eells, a full-time salary and establish permanent headquarters in Washington, D.C.

During World War II, the number of junior colleges declined. The state of Iowa was particularly hard hit, with fourteen of its twenty-seven junior colleges closing during the first year of the war.[5] Enrollment dipped as men and women contributed to the war effort, but they skyrocketed as the war drew to a close and veterans took advantage of the GI Bill, as many vets were attracted to the semiprofessional programs these colleges offered. By 1944–45, more than 250,000 students attended junior colleges.[6]

The 1947 report of the President's Commission on Higher Education, better known as the Truman Commission, is considered a watershed in the evolution of "junior" to "community" colleges. This six-volume report influenced thinking over the next decades on all of the following aspects of community college development:

- the place of two-year colleges in America's system of higher education;
- the imperative to create such colleges across the country;
- the need to develop paraprofessional and vocational education programs as well as collegiate curriculums and to make the educational needs of the community the primary reference point for these colleges; and
- for states to develop and support systems of locally controlled colleges.

The Truman report "pushed the two-year college into the forefront of American higher education."[7] Although the report certainly did not invent community colleges, it made them "a keystone of national educational policy and set the stage for the massive college growth of the next two decades."[8] Soon after the report was published, colleges began changing their names from "junior" to "community" colleges.

Indeed, the number of colleges and students doubled between 1960 and 1969.[9] More than 450 new colleges opened, leading to the oft-cited statistic that "a new community college opened every week" during this period. But as the number of public colleges grew, they drew students from their private college counterparts. In the 1960s alone, about one hundred private junior colleges closed or became baccalaureate-granting schools.[10] By 1970, there were some 850 public community or junior colleges; by 1980, a thousand. After that time, establishment of new colleges slowed considerably.[11]

Booming student enrollments drove this phenomenal period of building. In 1960, just over a half million students were attending junior and community colleges; by 1970, that number had doubled to more than two million. That number doubled once again, so that by 1980, four million students were attending.[12]

This huge influx of students is attributed to the expansion of the population between the ages of eighteen and twenty as a result of the post–World War II baby boom. Indeed, the age group of fifteen- to twenty-four-year-olds increased by 68 percent between 1955 and 1970.[13] By 1990, credit enrollments had risen to more than five million, with another four million in noncredit programs.[14]

Two of the women profiled in this book—Margaret Mosal and Mildred Montag—made their contributions while the colleges were still primarily junior colleges in number and mission.[15]

The majority of these women first made their mark during the booming 1970s. Despite its growing size and importance, this sector of higher education had not yet gained general acceptance or understanding in the minds of the public or the established higher education community.[16]

The women who were more visible in the late 1980s and early 1990s—Wilhelmina Delco, Janine Pease, and Barbara Bratone—made contributions that extended the reach of the movement with their vision of community colleges as places of expanded educational opportunity for African Americans and American Indians.

THE CHANGING SOCIAL CONTEXT FOR WOMEN

Though familiar and extensively documented, it is important to remember the societal and employment context confronting the women profiled in this book as they pursued their education and careers. They grew up in a world far different from that today's young women enjoy. Attending college after high school was the exception, not the rule. In 1960, only 8 percent of women had completed four or more years of college; by 1980, that number had risen to just 21 percent.[17] Women who attended college prepared for a narrow array of careers, largely in teaching, nursing, or clerical positions.

Those who chose to work, rather than become housewives, were in the minority, making up just 33 percent of the labor force in 1960. The workplace continued to reflect occupational segregation, with 80 percent of women holding "female" jobs. Women's earning power was substantially below that of their male counterparts. In 1960, women earned 60 percent of men's wages, in part due to their lower educational attainment levels.[18]

The disparities and frustrations of these inequities were highlighted in Betty Friedan's best-selling *The Feminine Mystique* in 1963, which is often credited with igniting the women's movement. Taking a page from the book of the civil rights movement, Friedan and others founded the National Organization for Women in 1966, for the purpose of "taking action to bring women into full participation in the mainstream of American society now, exercising all privileges and responsibilities thereof in truly equal partnership with men." Inclusion of the phrase "taking action" was purposeful, as the organization engaged in direct mass actions and intensive lobbying, grassroots political organizing, and litigation.

A parallel but more strident movement arose on college campuses, spearheaded by young college women frustrated by what they perceived as pervasive inequality of opportunity. Dubbed the "women's liberation" or "feminist" movement, these activists established battered women's shelters, rape crisis hotlines, campus childcare centers, and women's health care clinics.

Congress first acknowledged its responsibility for gender inequalities with passage of the Equal Pay Act in 1963, requiring most companies to pay equal wages regardless of sex to those performing equal tasks.

This was followed in 1964 with Title VII of the Civil Rights Act, which prohibited employment discrimination on the basis of sex, race, religion, and national origin. To enforce the law, Congress established the Equal Employment Opportunity Commission, which received fifty thousand sex discrimination complaints in its first five years. It wasn't until this act was revised in 1972 that colleges were required to eliminate discrimination in hiring.

Additionally, Title IX in the Education Code of 1972 prohibited discrimination on the basis of sex in education programs or activities by colleges and universities and other organizations receiving federal funds. Finally, in 1993, Congress passed the Family and Medical Leave Act, which mandated up to twelve weeks of unpaid leave for parents to care for newborns.

In addition to these legal protections, women, along with racial minorities, began to benefit from what were known as "affirmative action" policies, in which employers sought aggressively to identify, hire, and promote those previously discriminated against in the workplace. The corollary in higher education was affirmative action to recruit and admit women and minorities into higher education—particularly graduate and professional programs—in which they were underrepresented.

These enforceable rights—now practically taken for granted—were not guaranteed to any of the women profiled in this book when they were choosing where to go to college, what fields to study, and what jobs to seek after graduation. Yet most of them "came of age" professionally during the women's movement and found that their talents and ambition opened doors for them in a way not possible for women in the first half of the century.

During the decades of the movement's phenomenal growth (1960–1980), few names surface in the literature of female presidents who gained national prominence. An obvious explanation for this is that very few attained these platforms of influence prior to 1990. Although the data varies slightly by source, the trend is clear. In 1973, 5 female presidents of public two-year colleges were reported;[19] by 1982, only 21 women headed one of the more than one thousand colleges;[20] in 1984, 72;[21] and by the early 1990s, that number had risen to around 140.[22] By contrast, in 2016, some 387 women were listed in the AACC membership directory as presidents, chancellors, or chief executives of 1,108 colleges, representing more than one-third of all such positions.[23]

Additionally, Rossi reported in 1975 that although 24 percent of community college administrators were women, most were librarians and registrars.[24] Nearly all directors and officers of the American Association of Community and Junior Colleges were white males. No woman was elected as chair of that association board between 1952 and 1977. In short, female leaders were still the exception during the period covered in the profiles of this book.

EXPANDING ACCESS TO HIGHER EDUCATION

The 1960s and early 1970s marked an expansion of the notion of who should have access to a higher education. Although community colleges were in the forefront of offering access to previously underrepresented groups such as women, minorities, and the disabled, they did not lead these broad social movements, but rather mirrored them.[25] By the mid-1960s, "public leaders and national groups . . . singled out the community colleges as being the most logical and economical agency to provide needed educational opportunity beyond high school."[26]

Among the trends and types of "nontraditional" students who diversified the ranks of young, mostly white college students were:

Female students. In 1968, 36 percent of freshmen entering community colleges were female; by 1971, that number had risen to more than 41 percent.[27] Fueled by exhortations from the women's movement and expanding employment opportunities for women, these numbers continued to climb. Colleges started to respond to what were perceived as the unique needs of women by introducing women's centers and women's studies courses, childcare centers, and programs for "displaced homemakers." By 1980, females constituted more than half (55 percent) of community college students,[28] and have ever since.

Minority students. Originally, most junior colleges sprang up in small towns and rural communities. During the 1960s, colleges opened up in nearly every major metropolitan center. Following on the heels of the civil rights movement, African Americans began to enroll in greater numbers in two-year colleges.

By 1970, minority students—defined as African American, Chicano, Asian, and other—made up 14 percent of community and junior college enrollments.[29] To further social ends, the federal government designed numerous programs intended to benefit minority students and made funding available both for research studies and at the programmatic level.

Adult students. During the 1970s, the enrollment of older students swelled. As the baby boom cohort moved beyond traditional college age, colleges recognized this as a new market to replace the declining numbers of young people.[30] The concept of "lifelong learning" gained prominence, culminating in the passage of the federal Lifelong Learning Act, Title I-B of the 1976 Higher Education Amendments. Not until the mid-nineties, however, was education for mature adults viewed as an integral function of mainstream higher education. As the age of students went up, the number of credit hours each student attempted went down, shifting the percentage of students attending part-time from 47 percent in 1968 to 62 percent by 1980.[31]

Vocational students. Key to moving from the junior college to the community college model was the inclusion in the curriculum of occupational and technical programs. Coupled with the accelerating demands for trained technicians after World War II was the passage of the federal Vocational Education Act in 1963, which earmarked 20 percent of funding for community colleges.

In 1960, only one-quarter of all community college students were in occupational programs;[32] by 1975, that number had increased to more than one-third of all students.[33] Proliferation of technical trades and the availability of training for them in community colleges had the result of expanding access to a group of students—largely of a lower socioeconomic class—who heretofore had terminated their education with a high school diploma.

Students with special needs. By the early 1970s, the expansion of access resulted in "an increasingly large number of entering students who do not possess even minimal levels" of preparation.[34] Students in this category included those lacking basic college-level academic readiness, served by what colleges called "developmental education" courses and programs.

Other students who were labeled "culturally disadvantaged" required colleges to provide significant support services to ensure their success.

More students for whom English was a second language also enrolled. Additionally, colleges began to recognize that many students who had not been successful in schools were hindered by learning disabilities and physical handicaps and that accommodations were required.[35]

This brief overview sets the stage for the stories of the women selected for this book. Many of them focused their professional attention on the needs of these nontraditional student populations or on training those who were to lead in addressing their needs. Along with expanded access came a plethora of policy questions, political dynamics, and funding opportunities, and other of these women seized the opportunity to contribute in these arenas.

Part II

PROFILES

Chapter One

Margaret James Mosal

Champion for High-Achieving Students

Margaret James Mosal

Phi Theta Kappa, the international academic honorary society for two-year college students, is the oldest, largest, and most prestigious honor society recognizing students pursuing two-year degrees. Phi Theta Kappa has more than three million members and nearly thirteen hundred chapters in nine nations. Its roots date to 1918, when a group of presidents of women's junior colleges in Missouri saw the need to consolidate the various honor society chapters that were springing up around the state. The name Phi Theta Kappa was chosen to mirror the name and purpose of the baccalaureate-level Phi Beta Kappa Society.

The stated purposes of Phi Theta Kappa were to recognize academic excellence among two-year college students, to provide opportunities for leadership training, to provide an intellectual climate for the interchange of ideas and ideals, and to imbue scholars with the desire for continued education.

Soon, chapters were initiated in neighboring states, and by 1928, junior colleges in six states were included in the society. Wishing to enhance its prestige, the society drew up a petition to the American Association of Junior Colleges (AAJC) requesting recognition as the official honor society of two-year colleges. The request was granted at the AAJC's annual meeting in 1929.

ASSUMES LEADERSHIP POSITIONS
IN PHI THETA KAPPA

That same year, 1929, Margaret James had joined Phi Theta Kappa as a student while seeking her associate's degree at Whitworth Junior College in Brookhaven, Mississippi. In 1930, she was elected its first national president. After completing her degree, she married William Louis Mosal (Mo-zél) and moved to Canton, Mississippi. They became parents to a son, William, and a daughter, Mary Margaret.

In 1935, she ran for and was elected the national secretary of Phi Theta Kappa. At the time, seventy-two chapters were chartered in twenty states. Lacking a central office, the organization was run out of the national secretary's home base, which, in this case, was William Mosal's hardware store, located on the Square in Canton. This transition is characterized fondly as Margaret Mosal taking the organization's records home "in a shoebox."

Thus began Margaret's fifty-year career as chief executive (under various titles) of Phi Theta Kappa. As with any relatively new national organization, little funding for full-time staff was available. Margaret served as Phi Theta Kappa's only staff person, compensated at the rate of fifty dollars per month.

Left a widow at age forty-three when William died in 1954, Margaret found herself in need of a paying job. Without an advanced degree, her career options were limited. Fortunately, Charles Hogarth, president of the Mississippi College for Women, in Columbus, was acquainted with Margaret and hired her as the college's first transfer student admissions counselor. Although her children moved with her to Columbus, the demands of their mother's job were hard on them, and they asked to return to Canton, where Margaret arranged for live-in help in her absence.

Recognizing the pool of potential students from the state's junior colleges, the college expected Margaret to be on the road recruiting transfer students. This assignment dovetailed nicely with her Phi Theta Kappa responsibilities, as it kept her in touch with junior colleges throughout the state.

THE EARLY YEARS

Between 1935 and 1967, Margaret essentially ran Phi Theta Kappa on her own by leaning on volunteers and using an informal organizational structure. The society had little or no money, and she was operating in "a man's world."[1] She got people to support the organization during this period "by her determination, will, and great charm."[2] By 1967, the explosive growth of two-year colleges led the organization to recognize its need for a paid staff. Margaret became employed full-time as executive secretary (although she continued to work out of her home), and a formal board of directors was established.

By the early 1970s, Phi Theta Kappa purchased its first national headquarters—a house in Canton (around the corner from Margaret's home), which was turned into office space. As Phi Theta Kappa was a private organization, Margaret could hire whom she pleased on staff, and thus she chose to employ those she trusted most: her sister, her brother, and his wife. In 1977, Phi Theta Kappa moved to its first official office space with the purchase of the old home economics building of Canton High School.

With the tremendous growth in community colleges in the 1960s, Phi Theta Kappa reassessed its practice of having students join the society as they neared graduation. As nurturing organizations, community colleges strove to help develop potential in their students. Thus, it was decided that the society would be more than merely honorific and would recognize human potential by inviting students that had completed twelve credit hours or more who had earned a grade point average of 3.5 to join; then during their college years, the society would provide programming and opportunities that would help them grow and succeed.

SIGNATURE PROGRAMS INTRODUCED

Phi Theta Kappa's purpose rests on four "Hallmarks": Scholarship, Leadership, Fellowship, and Service. During Margaret's tenure, she helped develop programming that emphasized or reflected these hallmarks. A series of national awards was established, nurtured, and refined into the Hallmark Awards Program, still in use. The four major regions each came to be represented by a national vice president, and the separate society regions, with regional coordinators at the helm, were organized to represent the different states.

Despite the fact that her Phi Theta Kappa responsibilities entailed frequent travel, Margaret always used a car or train; she would not fly. It was, in fact, during a train ride to an AAJC convention in 1967 when she and her fellow travelers hatched the idea of an honors institute. The plan was to establish an institute where students would come together during the summer to study a timely interdisciplinary topic, chosen each year by selected faculty.

The first Honors Institute was held in 1968 on the campus of Endicott College, a private women's junior college outside Boston. Each year, students heard from nationally prominent speakers such as Henry Cabot Lodge, Beverly Sills, Eric Sevareid, H. R. Haldeman, and Alex Haley on a selected theme. Another key component of the Honors Institute exposed students to new cultural experiences. When the Honors Institute was held in Boston, for example, students would hear the Boston Pops, visit Plymouth Rock, and tour local historic sites.

Today, within honors programs circles, the Phi Theta Kappa Honors Institute is considered the premier program of its kind. Attendance is limited to five hundred students. The program is replicated in Phi Theta Kappa's twenty-nine regions, where, at Margaret's urging, colleges select the honor study topic as the foundation for interdisciplinary programs and activities back on campus. This allows students from throughout the country to experience a version of the Honor's Institute.

Further, Margaret enhanced *The Golden Key*, Phi Theta Kappa's magazine, and the annual Phi Theta Kappa convention, held each spring. Student chapters would work all year to raise money to attend, arriving in the selected convention city in buses, vans, and wagons. Initially held on college campuses, by 1968 the convention had grown so large that it began meeting in convention centers around the country.

Aubrey K. Lucas, then president of Delta State University and a long-time member of the Phi Theta Kappa board of directors, characterizes the conventions as wonderful occasions. "If you haven't been to one of those national meetings and seen what happens to those students . . . then you just don't know what [Margaret's] contribution was all about." He captures her contribution well:

> I was really taken with these bright students. Most of them were almost in poverty. They chose to attend junior or community colleges because of the cost, and they could drive to attend. So you have these bright, excelling people who for the first time in their lives were getting recognition. She really wanted to build their self-confidence and self-esteem and for them to understand their self-worth. If you could have seen how she related to those students! [It gave you] a wonderful feeling about yourself and others, and that's what so many of these students needed.[3]

ASSESSING A FIFTY-YEAR CAREER

As Margaret neared the fifty-year mark with the society, her health—physical and mental—was failing, but she was reluctant to turn over the leadership of this organization that had been her lifelong passion. She died in 1987, just two years after formally retiring as executive director.

Margaret Mosal's contribution to the community college movement is remarkable for several reasons. Her dedication to this single purpose spanned fifty years. She experienced the evolution from junior colleges to community colleges to the national phenomenon that they became. She never went further than the associate's degree in formal study, although she was awarded an honorary doctor of humanities from Pfeiffer College is 1972.

"We wouldn't have a Phi Theta Kappa if Margaret Mosal had not just stayed with it," believes Aubrey Lucas: "She was a builder, a persuader, and an organizer." The American Association of Community and Junior Colleges recognized her in 1985 with its prestigious AACJC Leadership Award—the first woman on whom that honor was bestowed.

The inclusion of Margaret Mosal on a list of influential women does not receive unanimous assent. Many activists in the movement do not recognize her name. This may be due to the fact that, as a former college president noted, "Phi Theta Kappa is kind of a small circle—just the students and faculty who are involved."[4] But just as high-risk students have been the beneficiaries of numerous special programs, projects, and funded initiatives, high-achieving community college students, too, deserve attention. Phi Theta Kappa chapters allow colleges to reward, recognize, and invest in students who excel. Further, as the chapters are governed by student members, the society gives students the opportunity for on-campus leadership positions.

Another observer was never convinced that Margaret "had a particular interest in the community-college philosophy."[5] Indeed, Margaret's perspective was on the individual, not on the institution. Her goal was to develop students' sense of self-worth and confidence. Many credit those who came *after* her with the growth and reputation of today's Phi Theta Kappa.[6]

PHI THETA KAPPA BENEFITS FROM LEADERSHIP OF OTHERS

David Pierce, former head of the American Association of Community Colleges, credits Margaret with making Phi Theta Kappa "one of the best run organizations on the planet."[7] He believes that she grew it into a strong, exceptional organization, and that director Rod Risley "took it to higher levels."

Rod Risley was hired by Margaret in 1977 and succeeded her as executive director (until 2015). He is credited with giving the organization greater national visibility through the annual recognition of the All-USA Academic Team of two-year college students in conjunction with *USA Today*, establishing its permanent headquarters in Jackson, Mississippi, and vastly expanding the society's membership and visibility.

Risley in turn praises the contributions of Shirley Gordon, one of the country's first female presidents, from Highline (Washington) Community College, who joined the Phi Theta Kappa board in 1986 and served as its chairman from 1988 to 2007. As chair, she was instrumental in designing a leadership program for community college students that earned a major grant from the Kellogg Foundation in 1991; with authorizing the first capital campaign, which led to the building of a permanent facility for the society (for which she suggested the name, the "Center for Excellence"); and with helping develop programming with the National Science Foundation to improve curricula in science, mathematics, engineering, and technology.

Shirley Gordon was also a major financial contributor to the society because of her strong belief in its mission. In 2005, Shirley received AACC's National Leadership Award in recognition for having "significantly advanced academic opportunity for students through her work with Phi Theta Kappa."[8]

Yet Margaret Mosal's spirit lives on forty years after her death. The international organization makes its home not at One Dupont Circle in Washington, but in Jackson, Mississippi, not far from her family home in Canton. At the International Convention, the Mosal Award, which carries a stipend of $5,000, is awarded to a Phi Theta Kappa adviser who makes significant contributions to the honor society, the college, and the local community through leadership and service.

IMPORTANCE OF THE PERSONAL TOUCH

Margaret's success in transforming Phi Theta Kappa International Honor Society into a highly regarded student-centered organization with five hundred chapters in forty-nine states by the time of her retirement is attributed to her skills as a communicator and to the decision to turn the organization from an honorific society to one that nurtured student growth and development. Everyone, once they had a chance to talk with Mrs. Mosal about Phi Theta Kappa, became convinced that it was important "just by the way she presented it."[9] As Rod Risley recalls,

> She was an incredible communicator but more so a motivator and one who understood how to empower people. People did things for her that they would not do for anyone else. She could get you to do so much for nothing except a big hug and knowing that what you did was so important.
>
> I stood witness so many times when she interacted with students, their advisers, and college presidents—she would engage in conversation with

that person, and for them, the world stood still for that moment. You almost didn't know what was happening. She made you feel you were the most important person in the world. As you believed in yourself, you were willing to do anything for her. You didn't want to let her down.[10]

During Margaret's reign, Phi Theta Kappa became known for its tradition of hugging. According to one of her former deputies, Margaret claimed that hugging was a quick and easy way for a woman to gracefully make her way through a crowd of important people, and they would be just as satisfied with a warm hug as with a long conversation.[11] Margaret Mosal was a "visionary who provided the foundation of what really mattered"[12] while always maintaining the personal touch.

Chapter Two

Mildred L. Montag

Innovator in Nursing Education

Mildred L. Montag

In the transition from "junior" to "community" colleges the Truman Commission on Higher Education envisioned a critical need: the development of terminal occupational programs. In the late 1940s, "we were having a hard time getting professional programs going in two-year colleges," recalls Edmund Gleazer, Jr., then president of the American Association of Junior Colleges. One woman—through careful argumentation, oversight, and research—introduced to community colleges one of its most ubiquitous and successful programs—the associate degree in nursing. It is no exaggeration to say that Mildred L. Montag "changed the course of nursing education in the United States."[1]

Born in 1908 in Struble, Iowa, to Joseph and Louise Montag, Mildred was the only member of her family to attend college. Although when younger she had toyed with the idea of becoming a nurse, by the time she attended Hamline University in St. Paul, Minnesota, she had drifted into preparing for a career teaching history.

As she approached graduation in 1930, the idea of a nursing career reemerged, especially when she learned of the University of Minnesota School of Nursing in neighboring Minneapolis. Her clinical experience at Minneapolis General Hospital, where the high standard of care was given to patients, regardless of "age, socioeconomic conditions, social status, color, and creed," heavily influenced Mildred's attitude about nursing care.[2]

Another important learning experience was the exposure Mildred received to a liberal education at Hamline and the University of Minnesota. When later she had the opportunity to fashion nursing education programs, first at Adelphi College in New York, and then when proposing the associate degree curriculum, she was insistent upon the importance of the liberal arts for prospective nurses. "I knew what liberal education would mean to students because it had meant so much to me."[3]

It appears that Mildred caught the eye of her professors and advisers along the way, as they encouraged her to pursue a master's degree in curriculum and teaching, then a doctorate in educational administration. With a scholarship, she was admitted to Columbia University for graduate study, quickly deciding on an emphasis in education at Teachers College (TC). The college by the 1940s had established a reputation as a pioneer in nursing education.[4]

Finding a source of income became necessary once she decided to pursue her doctorate. Having specialized in nursing education, Mildred found employment teaching at St. Luke's Hospital School of Nursing in New York City. This proved to be an eye-opener. She learned that schools of nursing trained their students in a way specific to that hospital, as their graduates constituted the pool from which they hired nurses. After brief employment as a nurse with the Henry Street Visiting Nurse Service and, later, with the Psychological Corporation, Mildred concluded that nursing education "was the right choice for me."[5]

In 1943, Mildred was hired as the founding director of the new nursing program at Adelphi College, established in response to the need for nurses for war services.[6] In implementing the program, she wanted it to be an integral part of the college, as she "believed strongly in the need for nursing education to be comparable to other educational experiences." By 1948, she turned her attention fully to her doctoral studies at Teachers College, where soon she was hired as a full-time instructor, and there she remained for the rest of her career.

REVAMPING NURSING EDUCATION

To many observers, the state of nurse training was in sorry shape. Nearly 83 percent of all schools of nursing were hospital-based; the other 18 percent were in university schools of nursing.[7] During their three-year training program, students were essentially a "captive labor pool."[8] Usually housed in proximity to the hospital, nurses-in-training became low-cost labor for hospitals, doing highly repetitive tasks, which limited their learning opportunities.[9]

In addition to classroom hours, they often worked forty-four to forty-eight hours per week, for which usually they were not compensated. Instead, they paid a nominal tuition. "It was becoming apparent to increasing numbers of people that it was an outmoded system."[10] Mildred observed in her dissertation, "Since the primary purpose of the hospital is the care of the sick, decisions must be made with that in mind. Thus the service demands of the hospital rather than the students' needs all too frequently determine the students' activities." Further, most programs did not allow older or married students.

At Teachers College, Mildred came to learn about junior/community colleges through her coursework, and she also had the good fortune to work under Dr. R. Louise McManus, a member of the TC nursing education faculty. Dr. McManus had proposed that "nursing functions were too broad and too complex to be encompassed by a single worker in nursing, and therefore should be differentiated. She proposed three categories on a continuum—complex (professional), intermediate (technical), and simple (assisting)."[11]

Mildred was uniquely poised to comment on the state of nurse training, having attended a liberal arts college and a university nursing school, directed both diploma- and university-based programs, practiced briefly as a nurse, and benefited from the tutelage of Dr. McManus. Taking her professor's idea one step further, Mildred proposed in her dissertation that the training for this middle level of practitioners—the technician—should be taken out of the hospital and brought into higher education. After reviewing where it might best be placed, she settled on two-year colleges.

> The community college, as seen by the President's Commission on Higher Education [1947] is recommended as the preferable institution because of its purpose, its location, and the variety of curricula it will offer.[12]

Importantly, she then went on to fashion an entirely new curriculum for the training of nurses, which could be completed in two years. Part would need to be devoted to general education, "designed to prepare the student for social and personal competency."[13] Specifically, students would study communications, sociology, economics, literature, U.S. history, and government.

Another emphasis would be courses "given to the development of skill in giving nursing care to patients,"[14] such as human biology, microbiology, human growth and development, nutrition, and the "nursing arts."[15] Clinical experience would round out the curriculum. This model curriculum "should be tried out and studied carefully"[16] with institutions offering this kind of program having "complete control of the entire curriculum, including the clinical experience."[17]

In other sections of her dissertation, Mildred recommended how the programs would be financed, what facilities should be used, how students should be selected, how the programs should be accredited, what this new associate degree might be called, and why the program would appeal to types of students previously unwilling or unable to attend hospital diploma programs. In short, Mildred "worked out the philosophy and plan for an entirely new kind of nursing program, developing at the same time the design for research that would test the viability of the idea."[18]

PROPOSED IDEA FOR NEW APPROACH
TO NURSING EDUCATION FINDS SUPPORT

This innovative proposal might have languished if it were not for its publication by G. P. Putnam & Sons in 1951. Released just prior to the 1950 convention of the National League of Nursing Education, it "caused quite a stir."[19] But the environment was ripe for seizing on Mildred's proposal. As early as 1946, the U.S. Office of Education, the National League for Nursing, the American Association for Junior Colleges, and the Association of Collegiate Schools of Nursing were all in their own way exploring the expanded uses of junior colleges for educating nurses.[20]

All of these groups were concerned with the shortage of nurses and with the perceived lack of professional training available in hospital-based programs. Mildred's well-laid out proposal for a nurse-technician educated in junior/community colleges seemed promising.

By 1948, both the Russell Sage and Kellogg Foundations were making significant grants to further the conversation. In 1950, the National League for Nursing had approached AAJC to form a committee to develop nursing education programs in two-year colleges. In part spurred on by the publication of Mildred's book, this committee recommended the initiation of two-year nursing degrees, established a national advisory committee for this purpose, and named Dr. Montag the project director.[21] With the generous help of a $110,000 gift from an anonymous donor,[22] the Cooperative Research Project (CRP) in Junior and Community College Education for Nursing was established.

With the assistance of Ed Gleazer and AAJC, seven diverse junior/community colleges and one hospital-based program were chosen as pilot sites. The CRP, initiated in 1952, had two controlling purposes: to define a new worker in nursing, the "technical" nurse; and then to design the educational preparation of this new kind of nurse. This nurse would be distinguished from other nurses by the scope of her practice, which would fall somewhere between those of the practical nurse and those of the traditional professional nurse who was being educated in baccalaureate programs.[23]

Although Mildred believed strongly that each project should be free to design and experiment within a general design, each was organized on a conception of nursing that was patient-centered, not disease-centered, which clearly distinguished them from traditional nursing education.[24]

Follow-up studies of program graduates were planned from the very beginning of the project. Of the 176 graduates who took licensing examinations, 91.7 percent passed on their first attempt, which compared favorably with those completing other types of programs.[25] Further, Mildred wrote in her summary report,

> With some experience, they are able to carry on the nursing functions as well as or better than the graduates of other types of programs.
>
> Applications consistently exceeded the number that could be admitted.
>
> Certain individuals who might otherwise not have been attracted to or able to attend another type of nursing school found there programs particularly desirable and accessible.[26]

By the time the project was completed in 1956, "there were more programs outside the project than within."[27] In fact, forty such programs were in operation by 1958, and many more were in the planning stage.[28] "The two-year nursing program not only caught on, it spread like wildfire."[29] By 1960, 40 junior and community colleges offered the associate's degree in nursing (ADN);[30] by 1967, 286;[31] by 1970, 600;[32] by 1978, 677;[33] and by 1990, more than 800.[34] "Programs doubled every four years between 1952–1974."[35]

CONVINCING STATE NURSING BOARDS

Although in general the nursing profession "did not take kindly to the idea,"[36] by project completion it was hard to argue with the dent in the nursing shortage these new programs were making. Soon, the Kellogg Foundation asked Mildred to direct the New York State Associate Degree in Nursing Project, which sought to accelerate the development of the associate degree in nursing in California, Florida, New York, and Texas—all of which were interested in a statewide approach to ADN education.

At the time, the nursing profession was regulated by boards of nursing state-to-state. In California, for instance, aspiring nurses were required to complete at least three years of training prior to licensure. Mildred saw it as part of her job to work with state legislatures and boards of nursing examiners to amend existing regulations. In fact, she spoke with state licensing boards in all of the states in which the CRP had pilot sites—New York, New Jersey, Michigan, California, and Virginia.[37]

Her commitment to seeing this innovation through carried well beyond the funding years. Mildred engaged in voluminous correspondence with educational institutions wishing to implement an ADN program.[38] Additionally, she traveled extensively as a consultant, met with the pilot colleges many times a year, and participated in the annual workshop of the faculty in the cooperating colleges.

The introduction of this highly successful career-oriented degree program "gave impetus to other technically related programs" in community colleges.[39] The way the program was developed served as "a model of how to use industry as a basis for developing a knowledge base."[40] Edmund Gleazer, Jr., then-president of AAJC, believes that "the ADN program became one of the prime movers in the development of semi-professional or technical programs in community colleges."[41]

LONG-TERM IMPACT OF MONTAG'S EFFORTS

Today, more than one thousand community colleges (the vast majority) offer associate degree programs in nursing,[42] and 55 percent of the first-time candidates for registered nurse licensing are products of these programs.[43] Unequivocally, "the ADN movement has been highly successful."[44]

Although clearly many were poised to move nursing into higher education, it is Mildred Montag who receives credit for making it happen—through her insights into what two-year colleges had to offer, the publication of her carefully reasoned dissertation, her willingness to direct the implementation project, her explicit research design focused on program outcomes, her vast consulting work, and her reasoned advocacy before state regulatory boards.

As a trained nurse, an excellent teacher,[45] a competent researcher,[46] and author of several highly popular textbooks for use in nursing programs,[47] Mildred's breadth of talent and accomplishments was remarkable. But of all of her achievements, she took the greatest satisfaction from hearing from individuals who credited these programs with changing their lives. "To think one has helped someone achieve a goal makes it all worthwhile."[48] Just six months after granting this author a telephone interview, Mildred L. Montag died at age ninety-five.

Chapter Three

Jane Elizabeth Matson

Mentor for Student-Development Personnel

Jane Elizabeth Matson

Few personalities from the sixties and seventies have their name so closely aligned with a single facet of community colleges as does Jane Elizabeth Matson with student personnel services. Although she retired in 1980 after twenty-two years as a professor with the Department of Counselor Education at California State University, Los Angeles, many people still have vivid recollections of the part that Jane played in shaping their careers and their vision of the role of student-services professionals.

Jane was born to well-educated parents in 1914 in Kirkwood, Illinois. Her father, Clyde Matson, was professor of music at the University of Chicago. Her mother, Mabel June Duram Matson, graduated from Monmouth College in Illinois. Jane's only sibling, a brother, died in infancy.

At a young age, Jane was selected as a subject in Dr. Lewis M. Terman's longitudinal study of children with IQ scores of 135 or over. The cohort of "Terman's little geniuses," as they were known, was contacted every five to ten years to gather data for life span research studies.

Little documentation remains from Jane's early years, but it is known that she received a BA in economics from the University of Chicago, worked after college for three federal agencies as a vocational counselor, and in 1946 joined the U.S. Navy's WAVES (Women Accepted for Voluntary Emergency Service), serving two years of active duty. Returning to college on the G.I. Bill, she completed an MA and EdD in counseling from Stanford University. She continued her affiliation with the U.S. Navy as a reservist, retiring after twenty years with the rank of captain.

INTRODUCED TO COMMUNITY COLLEGES

Jane's first professional position after graduate school was at Orange Coast College in Costa Mesa, California. Norm Watson, then chancellor of the Coast Community College District, remembers her as an excellent counselor, particularly effective with students who wanted to go on for a baccalaureate. Before long, a friend from graduate school, Leland Medsker, hired her for a counseling job at Diablo Valley College, where he was then president.

Lee Medsker's effect on Jane's career can only be surmised, as both are deceased. But clearly Jane went into the program at Stanford without a background in community colleges and came out of that experience a lifelong advocate of this nascent institution. One suspects the importance of Lee Medsker's influence, as he had already established a junior college in Chicago and was serving as founding president of Diablo Valley. They remained lifelong friends, with Medsker's active involvement in the community college movement while professor at the University of California, Berkeley, and director of its Center for Research and Development in Higher Education.

In 1958, Jane was hired by Los Angeles State College of Arts and Sciences as assistant professor in the counseling education department, with an emphasis on community colleges. Eventually obtaining tenure and promotions to full professor, Jane remained at what evolved into California State University, Los Angeles, until her retirement.

Unlike many university professors, Jane's reputation did not derive from her scholarly research. In fact, her publications were limited to a few pieces she wrote summarizing the state of student personnel services in community colleges. Cal State LA had no doctoral program, and it did not emphasize research and writing. Jane was more interested in networking, speaking, and training leaders.

STUDENT PERSONNEL INSTITUTE FOUNDED

From 1965 to 1973, Jane capitalized on the federal government's push for counselor training to encourage student interest in the sciences and mathematics by securing a series of grants through the National Defense Education Act (NDEA; later replaced by the Education for Professional Development Act), part of the Higher Education Act. Initially, NDEA was intended to focus on high school counseling, but the burgeoning of community colleges during that era made them an attractive venue for the federal government's education-based attempt to keep up with the Soviet Union in the *Sputnik* race.

With the funding, Jane established the Student Personnel Institute for Junior College and Technical Institute Personnel, one of eighteen such institutes in the United States. She ran the institute until 1973, when federal funding ran out.

Cal State LA's master's of science program in counselor education served part-time students working in the Los Angeles area. Jane's institute, on the other hand, was intended to attract a carefully selected group of thirty professionals willing to forgo employment for a year to concentrate on community college counseling. "She had people from all over the U.S. participating," recalls one former student. "They came from the East Coast, the West Coast, the interior, the South and the Northwest."[1]

"She picked the best and brightest," recalls Dick Alfred. "She had an influence on who entered into the field and who would ascend to leadership positions. She hand-picked people, giving special attention to people on their way up."[2] Others characterized her selection as her "screening service"[3]; she "plucked" us;[4] "she decided that I was a 'comer'—a term she liked to use. She was a king/queen maker."[5]

Mike Rooney, one of Jane's protégés, who went on to top leadership positions in several community colleges, tells a story of meeting Jane while attending a leadership institute in Hawaii. Jane was hired as a consultant to this institute because the organizers believed they had a better chance of securing federal funding if Jane was affiliated with their program. After one intensive twenty-four-hour "encounter group" session, Mike (an attendee) recalls,

> [Jane Matson] came up to me and put her hand on my shoulder, and said, "Man, I'm proud of you. What are you going to do with yourself and your career?" I said that I had no idea. She would not accept that. She looked at me with her piercing eyes and said, "Young man, I'm serious. I have this institute and we're going to be funded again, and I'd like to encourage you to participate. This [Hawaiian workshop] is good, but mine is great."[6]

And so Mike joined Jane's institute in Los Angeles, where he finished his master's degree.

In addition to taking courses toward a master's degree, students had the opportunity to participate in the institute's rich extracurricular offerings. With generous funding through the NDEA, Jane brought in a "galaxy of speakers," recalls John Davitt, one of her students. "She knew the movers and shakers—James Wattenbarger, Marty Martorana, Joseph Fordyce, Terry O'Banion, Dorothy Knoell. She brought them in as speaker[s] and consultants. We got to associate with them, they spent time with us."[7]

PROFESSIONALIZING STUDENT
SERVICES GOES NATIONAL

This group, along with others such as Alice Thurston, Dale Tillery, and Max Raines, formed a tight-knit friendship and support group. Jane was particularly close to Joe Fordyce, founding president of Santa Fe Community College in Florida. "Joe and Jane were the ringleaders."[8] Jane and Joe "turned me into a community-college advocate," says Terry O'Banion. "They introduced me to all the famous people."[9] People describe this group of colleagues as mutually reinforcing of each other. They mentored Jane Matson, and she, in turn, influenced them.

Jane and her cohorts actively promoted two-year colleges on the national scene. A group who regularly attended the annual ACPA/APGA (American College Personnel Association/American Personnel and Guidance Association) convention gathered in 1962 to organize a special committee to represent the interests of junior colleges.

Officially recognized by the ACPA Leadership Council in 1964 as Commission XI and titled "Junior College Student Personnel Services," Joe Fordyce served as its first president, Jane Matson as its second from 1965 to 1967. Under her leadership, the ACPA Commission XI became an affiliate of the American Association of Junior Colleges.

In 1966, AAJC president Edmund J. Gleazer, Jr., invited Jane to serve as specialist in student personnel work to implement recommendations from a study of ways to improve training for student personnel work. She moved to Washington, D.C., for two years, leaving her assistant director, John Davitt, in charge of the institute.

In 1970–71 she again joined AACJC to direct an Exxon Educational Foundation-sponsored follow-up study of two-year college student personnel programs, culminating in an article in the *Junior College Journal*. "One of her goals was to identify outstanding programs and concepts around the country and then to try to link other people up with them. She was a one-person clearinghouse."[10]

During 1976–77, Jane took another leave of absence from the university to be a consultant to community and junior college programs at the Educational Testing Service in Princeton, New Jersey. Her close friend Joe Fordyce, who was working at the College Board, arranged for Jane to go to Princeton. While there, she designed a workshop on the status of community colleges, which was so successful that subsequently it was offered in several other cities, coordinated by Dick Alfred, who at the time was with New York City Community College.

FROM "STUDENT PERSONNEL"
TO "STUDENT DEVELOPMENT"

Jane is one of the people credited with changing the thinking from "student personnel services" to "student development" during this era. Although most acknowledge that others such as Terry O'Banion were more in the forefront of this movement, Jane definitely saw counseling as more than "test 'em and tell 'em." Student-services staff should be trained in the behavioral sciences so they could enhance students' cognitive, social, and emotional development—in conjunction with academic faculty.

This approach was best exhibited at Santa Fe Community College, under Joe Fordyce, where "houses" were created that included faculty and counselors. There, counselors such as Max Bassett, a graduate of Jane's program, became consultants to faculty by observing what was happening in the classroom and advising them about communication and discipline issues.

Before these leaders began to rethink student services, "we were largely junior colleges, with student personnel meaning admissions and registration. Jane offered a larger conceptual framework for student services and how we think about them."[11] "She was one of the most important people in the field of student counseling that we've had," believes James Wattenbarger.[12] Robert McCabe gives her credit for

> bringing student affairs into focus as an integral part of an educational program in community colleges. Around that time, there was a rush to think that colleges had a responsibility for student performance, and you needed support services that dealt with the individual needs as well as their academic needs. This was a big insight, because until then it was expected that students were kind of on their own.[13]

"There was a lot of just taking someone who could not teach well and making them a counselor. She made student personnel work, especially counseling, into a professional track. For a long time, especially in southern California, her graduates populated many leadership positions. But NDEA students also fanned out to colleges around the country," says John Davitt.[14]

Jack Popeck is one who exemplifies the mentoring role Jane played in her students' lives. She took a liking to him when he moved from Wisconsin to join the institute in 1968 and increasingly gave him responsibilities. She linked him up with Jim Wattenbarger at the University of Florida, where she encouraged Jack to go for his doctorate.

Attending the AACJC convention while finishing graduate school, Jack learned of an opening for a coordinator of counseling services at

Northern Virginia Community College (NVCC). Once there, Jack helped implement the decentralized counseling model that Jane had promoted so strongly. That model, where counselors are assigned to each instructional division and spend time in classrooms, was still in place at NVCC's Alexandria campus in 2014. "She was convinced to the nth degree of the efficacy of the community-college counselor, that it was *integral* to the success of community colleges. Success was more than academic; it had to be accompanied by strong community-college counseling. She promoted the decentralized approach, a cooperative relationship between the academic and counseling. Counselors should be considered faculty. She believed in effective counseling programs."[15]

A MENTOR AND FRIEND

More than simply offering tremendous learning opportunities for her institute students, Jane became personally and professionally invested in their futures. The word that comes up repeatedly is "mentor." "She was on the phone for hours with people she felt had promise and talent."[16] Many people say that Jane "adopted" them, and, often, their families, too. The term "mother" is also used. "She followed up with her 'children,'" says Connie Sutton-Odems. "Up until her death, she was encouraging. We all loved and respected her."[17]

This mentoring had its downsides, however. After Richard C. Richardson began to focus his research interests outside community colleges, "she regarded me as a turncoat," although they remained on cordial terms.[18] "She was very strong in her opinions and was never reticent to express them. She adopted some of us to the extent that she could almost smother you—what jobs you could take and that kind of thing."[19]

People who knew her use oppositional descriptors. "Crusty as hell, but loyal as anyone could be."[20] "Tough as nails, then sweet as can be."[21] "A very complex person."[22] "She was very opinionated, would tell you what she liked and didn't like, and whether she liked someone or not. She was like a mother."[23] "When I first met Jane, I thought, 'Ohhh . . . a formidable woman, very businesslike, very stern, very focused.' But then after a time we got to know each other, and she became very human. She was a lot of fun."[24]

From all accounts, Jane remained devoted to her mother, who lived with Jane until her death at ninety-three. Both were active in La Cañada Presbyterian Church, where Jane served as a deacon. Mother and daughter often traveled together. She also toured widely with friends Dorothy Knoell and Alice Thurston, both of California.

Beyond that, "she had a huge family. There were all kinds of people who saw her as family and were inspired by her."[25] "Jane was very people-oriented. She needed people around her and quickly made friends wherever she went."[26] She became particularly close to John Davitt, his wife, Gael, and their children. When he became president of Glendale Community College near Jane's home in California, they became so close that "she treated our kids like her own."[27]

Jane did not slow down in her retirement from California State University in 1980. She joined up with Nova Southeastern University, where, as adviser to the EdD Program for Higher Education, she directed dozens of applied-research projects. She took great pride in her role with that nontraditional institution. She spent her winters in a home she purchased in Sun City; the rest of the year, she lived in the family home in La Cañada until two years before her death from leukemia in 1996.

Jane's commitment to community colleges is intriguing, given her acknowledged intellect, her superb educational training, and her upbringing in a university family. Some speculate that she was driven by "a real desire to make counselors and student personnel workers into professionals." It is possible that the community college movement appealed to her progressive, liberal political attitudes. In any case, she clearly had a strong belief in the value-added possibilities of community colleges and in the integration of the academic and personal progress of students as they moved through their college experience.

Chapter Four

Dorothy M. Knoell

Respected Researcher

Dorothy M. Knoell

When asked to name influential women in the community college movement from 1960 to 1990, people insist that the name of Dorothy M. Knoell
be included. All agree that no one provided more valuable contributions
as a researcher than did Dorothy—even though they associate her with
different seminal lines of research.

For many, her work with Lee Medsker on the transfer function in
the early 1960s is key; to others, it was her efforts in the late sixties to
increase opportunities for urban disadvantaged youth; and for others, it
was her work at the California Postsecondary Education Commission in

the mid-seventies where she documented the increasing heterogeneity in the student population of community colleges. In any case, Dorothy's research, projects, and publications spanned nearly three decades and were of national import.

As Dorothy neared high school graduation in 1939 in Patchogue, a small town on Long Island, New York, she realized that she "just wanted to get out of there,"[1] and that the best way out was to go to college. Her high school principal "made sure that male graduates went to college" but apparently had little interest in helping female students. The first in her family to consider college, she also was one of the few females in the graduating class with that desire.

Fortunately, she found an advocate in a female vice principal who, when she found out about Dorothy's aspirations, identified Douglass College in New Brunswick, New Jersey,[2] and helped find scholarships for her to attend. At Douglass, Dorothy majored in French, then continued on to the University of Connecticut, where she earned a master's in teaching of foreign languages.

Although she had an offer to teach in one of the best schools in the state, she could not see herself going into a high school and teaching foreign languages. She was curious about how higher education worked, but in 1945 no such field of graduate study existed, and there were no related jobs. So after a brief stint with the Girl Scouts in Yonkers, she jumped at an offer from the University of Connecticut to take a position in its testing bureau.

A PROFESSOR'S LETTER LEADS
TO GRADUATE SCHOOL

Knowing her continuing interest in graduate study, her major professor at Connecticut wrote a letter to the dean of the School of Education at the University of Chicago. He said he knew of a young woman who would like to pursue her doctorate and he would like to recommend her. The dean wrote back and offered Dorothy a job as his research assistant while she pursued her doctorate in research and evaluation, and Dorothy relocated to Chicago.

Her doctoral study consisted primarily of participating in her professors' research projects. She took some courses in statistics, but completing the doctorate entailed preparing for and passing the comprehensive exams, and writing a dissertation. After finishing the dissertation, which was on its Indian education, she had to work another year to pay for American typing. She was awarded the PhD in research and evaluation in 1948.

Although still desirous of doing educational research, she did not find herself drawn to vocational, adult, or teacher education—which were the major foci of doctoral study at that time. What held her interest were questions about college students and higher-education policy. So for about ten years she worked in various research-related jobs at the University of Wisconsin (doing postdoctoral work on verbal skills in American Indian children), in Texas (as an Air Force civilian research psychologist), and Pennsylvania (with the University of Pittsburgh's Schools of the Health Professions).

BECOMES DRAWN TO
EDUCATIONAL POLICY DEVELOPMENT

Finally in 1956, she was offered a research job in the state college unit of the California State Department of Education. She found the work fascinating; after working through issues with advisory groups, the staff took matters to the Council of Presidents, then to the State Board of Education. For the first time, Dorothy was watching the development of educational policy and loving it.

Then, in the late 1950s, she and her colleagues were assigned to assist the committee on the 1960 Master Plan for Higher Education. She helped staff the admissions and retention task force, which recommended the by-now well-known differentiation of admissions pools for the three segments (university, state colleges, and junior/community colleges). The Master Plan also made commitments to universal access through open-admissions to two-year colleges, free tuition, and support for the transfer function by assuring spaces in the other two segments for qualified community college students.

In short, the Master Plan "saw community colleges as the place for the majority of students." When it was adopted by the state legislature as the Donahoe Higher Education Act of 1960, among other things it established the California State College system, which moved the old system (and its staff) out of the jurisdiction of the State Board of Education.

Around that time, Leland L. Medsker, of the Center for Higher Education at the University of California, Berkeley, had become familiar with Dorothy's work and contacted her about working on a federal grant for which he needed someone to head up a nationwide study of the transfer function, including performance of transfer students and articulation between two- and four-year colleges. Intrigued, Dorothy moved to Berkeley and started the study.

> [It was a] marvelous opportunity for me. It gave me an entrée into the whole world. I would have been stuck forever in an office somewhere. No one knew me at the time. When you work for the state, you don't publish; nothing ever has your name on it.

LANDMARK STUDY ON THE
TRANSFER FUNCTION PUBLISHED

After nearly four years, she and Lee Medsker finalized *Factors Affecting Performance of Students from Two- to Four-Year Colleges* and *Articulation Between Two- and Four-Year Colleges*,[3] which was followed shortly by a widely distributed American Council on Education monograph, *From Junior to Senior College: A National Study of the Transfer Student.*[4]

This latter publication is now recognized as a landmark study on articulation.[5] The database used in the research included more than 7,000 students, 345 two-year institutions where they entered as freshmen, and a diverse group of 43 senior colleges to which they transferred. The authors analyzed the relationships between student characteristics, academic performance, and institutional and state differences.

Significantly, their research concluded that "Sixty-two percent of the junior college students were granted their baccalaureate degrees within three years after transfer and 9 percent were still enrolled at the beginning of the fourth year." This finding established what Dorothy has always considered to be more important than grade-point average changes or comparisons with "native" students: whether transfer students successfully complete a bachelor's degree.

Under President Edmund Gleazer's leadership, the AACJC was awarded a grant to hold state and regional conferences on the results of these studies and their implications for admissions, counseling, curriculum, instruction, and interinstitutional articulation. As Dorothy notes, it was "a unique study. It was not something you published and simply put on the shelf."

She relocated to State University of New York (SUNY) headquarters in Albany, getting the state conferences organized, speaking, and participating in discussions. This work coincided with the era when states were heavily engaged in master planning for higher education. James Wattenbarger, who served as the chair of the interorganizational committee that spawned the Knoell-Medsker study, credits this work, in part, with leading states such as Florida to develop specific policies relating to transfer.[6]

The significance of this study and its follow-up activities was not lost on those in the junior college movement. "She was one of the first people from the university side who saw the value and began to talk about the importance of community colleges from the academic side. Prior to Dorothy Knoell, not many [university] people were paying attention to community colleges and were willing to look at what they were doing," relates Robert McCabe.[7] "Her timing was perfect," says K. Patricia Cross, "because people were beginning to question the standards of community colleges. That [Knoell and Medsker] proved otherwise was really a breakthrough."[8]

ROLE FOR COMMUNITY
COLLEGES IN URBAN OUTREACH

Soon, Dorothy was offered another intriguing opportunity. Nelson Rockefeller, then governor of New York, and Samuel B. Gould, SUNY chancellor, were concerned that disadvantaged city youth had very limited opportunities for postsecondary education. The governor called for a study to determine whether there was need for another segment of postsecondary education to serve urban disadvantaged youth. Dorothy was asked to conduct the study during 1965–66.

The report's conclusions led to the establishment of centers in disadvantaged neighborhoods, under contract with community colleges. Dorothy

felt highly gratified by this project, as she saw it result in opening college
opportunity for those previously excluded.

> I was never actively involved in affirmative action per se for racial and
> ethnic minorities, but I think it was a first major outreach to urban disadvan-
> taged, who happened to be minorities—in most cases, black. The community
> colleges were simply not attuned to addressing those populations, so I think
> it was a major breakthrough in trying to get them to. We found in some of the
> new centers people with tremendous potential who had never had an oppor-
> tunity to do anything with higher education. This effort was not aimed at af-
> firmative action, but it did serve new populations that were heavily minority.

Dorothy's published work during this period in the mid-sixties, *Toward
Educational Opportunity for All*,[9] has been called "seminal."[10] "Knoell
envisioned a 'changing' society that would require increasing levels
of formal education of all its citizens because to limit access to higher
education on the grounds of outmoded notions of class and ability would
effectively exclude large numbers of youth . . . from participation in this
new economic order."

She saw the community college as the institution best able to accom-
modate this worthy population. Robert Pedersen further credits her work
with providing "a reasoned basis for the dramatic expansion of the City
University of New York's reliance on the community."[11]

Following this study, SUNY allowed Dorothy to go to its Washington
office for a year to develop a national project based upon the results. At
that time the U.S. Office of Educational Opportunity (OEO) was a highly
prominent agency. Mary Robinson, a senior staff member, was "totally
committed" to community colleges and had "untold funds" to award to
demonstration projects.

OEO funded Dorothy's work, known as the Urban Community College
project, at AACJC to go around the country and try to interest community
colleges in urban areas in developing similar projects for disadvantaged
adults and young people. She saw her role as a facilitator, working with
colleges that had potential for developing such programs.

She also had Ford Foundation support to work with high schools in cities looking at college attendance rates by race, comparing black and white
students on various criteria. It was an exciting time for her, but it was on

soft money. She keenly wanted to return to California, where the community colleges recently were reorganized under a new state governing board.

RETURNS TO CALIFORNIA FOR
POSITIONS WITH EDUCATION BOARDS

Then-chancellor Sidney Brossman recruited Dorothy heavily, as she had
a national reputation by this time, and she returned to California in 1969
as a curriculum specialist for the Chancellor's Office. She enjoyed the
governing board members but felt that it was not a good fit for her.

Soon, she was asked to move to the state coordinating agency to
conduct a legislatively mandated follow-up study of community college
students. In the course of the study, she visited each of the thirty colleges.
Afterward, "my friends at the Coordinating Council were able to slip me
into a position on the staff of the new CPEC [California Postsecondary
Education Commission]."

CPEC was Dorothy's home for the next twenty-three years, until her
retirement in 1994. As a chief policy analyst, she took great satisfaction
in conducting studies that commission members and other policy makers
"could understand and do something about."

She liked being close to the action, as the commission was conducting studies that led to changes in policy. For instance, in 1976, CPEC
published *Through the open door: A study of patterns of enrollment and
performance in California's community colleges.*[12] The report, which
Dorothy wrote, questioned the adequacy of conventional academic clas-
sifications and categories, such as attrition, dropout, transfer, and degree-
oriented. "Part-time students now comprise two-thirds of the headcount
enrollment," it reported. The dominant function of California's community colleges had become serving these part-time, adult students, "with
no resultant neglect of the occupational, transfer, and general education
functions of more traditional students."

This study, and Dorothy's subsequent works along the same lines,[13]
"helped me think about community college students and how they moved
in and out of our colleges and to senior institutions," recalls Alfredo de
los Santos of Maricopa Community College.[14]

Patrick M. Callan, who served as CPEC's director during Dorothy's most productive years there, believes that she had "a deep passion for community colleges, but also an ability to bring a critical perspective. Although she took heat and grief from the field, they understood that she raised important issues, and in a courageous way. She had the ability to understand [the colleges] from the inside but was able to view them from the outside."[15]

As someone "in the field," Paul Elsner, longtime chancellor of the Maricopa Community College District, agrees. "The movement was doctrinaire and defensive about what we were doing. Dorothy offered the first breath of empirical, quantitative [analysis]—'Why don't you ask and answer some questions about this movement once in a while?' She injected a bit of scientism in our movement that was sorely lacking."[16]

Whether or not people agreed with her, she earned their respect. She conducted "hard, analytic research with solid methodology and strong recommendations."[17] Yet people appreciated that she was "so practical and applied in her research."[18] "There was nobody whose data were more reliable and whose analysis about the transfer function was more credible. She tied world-class research skills to a values system where the research topics that she cared about were about educational opportunities for all," believes Alison Bernstein of the Ford Foundation.[19]

In the early years, says Pat Callan, "community colleges were not considered fully in the fold of higher education. But Dorothy brought credibility to research on community colleges as part of the policy discussions. She could speak the language *and* do the research."[20] Because she was not in the employ of the community colleges, her research and opinions often carried more weight than someone from the chancellor's office.

Dorothy's relationship to the leadership in the movement at that time was interesting. She could be counted on to appear at important community college meetings and conferences, often presenting her current research. A "tireless participator,"[21] "she knew everybody."[22] Many considered Dorothy a personal friend but were often annoyed at her for the vexing questions she raised and the opinions that she freely shared. Bernie Luskin, president of Coastline Community College, calls her "the little voice in your ear"[23] from that era. Her greatest contribution was "expressing her opinion."[24]

When asked why she thought she was good at research and analysis, Dorothy replied, "Because I'm not too abstract. I tried to do research that people would understand, simple things. I never tried to impress people with statistical analyses. I'd rather do something I could communicate to people; things leading to policy. I liked what my dean at Chicago would say: that research needed 'social validity,' not just 'statistical validity.'"

THE TRANSFER FUNCTION, REVISITED

Improving the transfer function continued as her research focus until retirement, culminating in her final significant work in 1990, *Transfer, articulation and collaboration twenty-five years later.*[25] In this report, funded by the Ford Foundation, she reviewed the viability of the transfer function over the two-and-a-half decades that spanned her research on this topic. The report concludes with a set of National Guidelines for Transfer and Articulation. Increasingly, Dorothy—and most others in the movement—had come to look toward state-level policy and programs to address continuing challenges to successful student transfer.

Throughout her career, Dorothy remained firm in her belief that a primary function of community colleges ought to be transfer. More than anything, these colleges served those who may not succeed in the first year at a university to help them succeed and transfer.

I am interested in the tremendous potential of young people. We [community colleges] do a far better job of instruction than in large university classes. I'm on the soapbox daily with young people about starting there.

Although her busy career dominated Dorothy's time, she took great enjoyment in travel abroad with professional colleagues and friends from her church. She passed away in 2011.

Chapter Five

Marie Y. Martin

Federal Advocate

Marie Y. Martin

The U.S. Department of Education's Title III Part A Programs (Strengthening Institutions) of the Higher Education Act has been the source of enormous seed money for community colleges, with tens of millions allocated annually to worthy three-year proposals.[1] But until an official inside the U.S. Office of Education advocated for allowing two-year colleges to receive money under this program in 1974, this source of funding was largely unavailable to them. That woman—who worked largely behind the scenes to make this happen—was Marie Y. Martin.

—⊷⊶⊷—

Only spotty records remain of the early years of Marie Young. What is known is that she was born in 1911 in Peterborough, Ontario, Canada, and received her BA in English from the University of California, Berkeley, in 1930. After her graduation, the UC Berkeley alumni office records her as working as a stenographer in the office of admissions.

The next public record of her appears in 1946, when her name appears as Marie Y. Martin in the catalog of L.A. City Colleges as a member of the business faculty, as a holder of a master's degree from the University of Southern California. The years between Berkeley and Los Angeles may have been spent obtaining her graduate degree and at home, as Marie is known to have married and had a son, Bill.[2]

Her teaching discipline at L.A. City College is listed as secretarial science. One wonders about these early years for Marie—graduating during the Depression from what was even then a prestigious institution of higher education, and ending up working as a stenographer and later teaching secretarial science! Her options do begin to open up when she completed her doctorate in education from the University of Southern California in 1954; the following year she joined L.A. City College's administrative ranks as assistant dean of instruction, and two years later (1956), dean of educational services.[3]

AN EARLY FEMALE PRESIDENT

In 1962, Marie began the first of three presidential appointments at other colleges in the Los Angeles Unified School District. She served as interim president at Valley College, and between 1962 and 1966, as president of Los Angeles Metropolitan College. In 1966, at age fifty-five, Marie was named president of Los Angeles Pierce College, the largest of the two-year colleges within the L.A. Unified School District.

This appointment made Marie one of the country's earliest female community college presidents. In an interview with the student newspaper upon her appointment, President Martin reflected upon the differences between Los Angeles Metropolitan College and her new assignment. In contrast to Metropolitan College, which drew students from all over southern California, Martin described Pierce as "a community college," by which she meant, "a college set up to give the students in a community easy access to the first and second years of academic, occupational, and technical training."[4] Apparently, the meaning of "community college" still required definition as late as 1966. The newspaper also reports that Dr. Martin was widowed.

Marie's years at Pierce were eventful ones, including seeing it become part of the newly formed Los Angeles Community College District; the closing of all California campuses in spring 1970 by order of Governor Ronald Reagan due to the "highly emotional conditions" prevailing from antiwar protests; and the attendant lists of demands, sit-ins, and other nonviolent student protests. (Marie seems to have managed this challenge with a steady hand, issuing a "go home or go to class" ultimatum to rallying students); and her own transfer in fall 1970 to a "president-at-large" position reporting to the district chancellor.[5]

TAKES NEW POSITION IN WASHINGTON, D.C.

Soon thereafter, Marie relocated across the country to Washington, D.C. At about that time, a group of community college trustees had pushed for the establishment of a separate office within the U.S. Department of Health, Education, and Welfare that recognized community colleges.[6]

Possibly because of the presence of Joseph Cosand (founding president of St. Louis Junior College District) as deputy commissioner for higher education at the U.S. Office of Education (1972–1973), the community college unit was formed, which was quite a feat as "the Office of Education didn't really want to acknowledge that it had a 'sector' person, because it was organized by function."[7] Marie Y. Martin was named as an early, if not its first, director.

Although details are sketchy, several sources describe Marie as having had a parting of ways with the American Association of Community and Junior Colleges and instead befriending the leadership of the recently formed Association of Community Colleges Trustees (ACCT). "Marie Martin kind of took me and ACCT under her wing," says William (Bill) Meardy, its longtime executive director, "and got us the money for the ACCTion program."

Along with being an early female president, Marie's role in initiating and funding what came to be known as the ACCTion Consortium is generally regarded as one of the most important single contributions by an individual during this era. Don Garrison, then president of Tri-County Technical College (SC), tells of its beginnings:

Around 1972, I went to a seminar at Duke University and became acquainted with Marie Martin. Soon after, she called and asked me to come to D.C. to meet with a group she had handpicked to discuss needs that community colleges had in faculty and staff development. There were about twenty of us there. We brainstormed. We had the two days to figure out what community colleges needed from Congress for money.

At the time, most Title III money was going to historically black college[s] and senior colleges. I shared the idea of surveying all Title III-eligible institutions and asking them what their needs were. After identifying the priority areas, we would form a consortium. Marie Martin did the research, and then called me and four other college representatives (from Kirkwood Community College, Brevard Community College, Hesston College, and San Diego Community College)[8] together a month later.

The presidents of these colleges and their grant persons met at the Kansas City airport, and Marie laid out the five top areas that were identified, and told the colleges to identify which area they would be responsible for; we each then provided our grants person, and they wrote a Title III proposal.[9]

Recalls Mike Crawford, then the development officer at Kirkwood Community College:

We [the grant writers] always went back to Marie Martin to make sure we were moving in the right direction. We met in San Francisco [1974] because that is where NCRD [National Council for Resource Development] was holding a meeting of its board. The idea was that we would meet with this experienced group of people on the NCRD board and they would help us write the grant proposal.

Our group met, and Marie was there with us. We quickly realized that the NCRD board was not going to help us but wanted to make [the idea] their own. I'll never forget having a drink in the bar with one of the NCRD board members, and he leaned over and told me, 'You're in the big leagues now, bubby.'

I went up to Marie Martin's room—she was not a young woman at the time—[she was] very tough. She was sitting in her room rocking on a rocking chair and giving me direction of what to do. We decided we could not work with NCRD; so the college representatives from the five colleges who were there to write the grant met in my room, we ordered room service and tables and chairs, locked the door, and wrote the grant.[10]

FEDERAL FUNDING FOR COMMUNITY COLLEGES

Crawford believes that Marie had the ear of Ernest Boyer, the U.S. commissioner of education. She convinced him that there should be a consortium to aid developing community colleges, just as there already were consortia for historically black colleges and universities and small independent colleges. The ACCTion Consortium did receive $1 million that next year and continued to be funded for an additional six years.

The theme of the project was "People helping People; Colleges helping Colleges." Only those colleges qualifying as "developing institutions" under Title III were eligible to apply for membership. Some 150 colleges were members over the life of the grant, from Maui Community College in Hawaii to Westbrook College in Portland, Maine.

Colleges chose one of the four components (community service, instructional services, resource development, or student development services) to work on for three years. After three years, colleges were required to change to another priority area. Although new colleges could join each year if there was attrition, the consortium maintained an 88 percent continuation rate.

All funds flowed from the Office of Education to four "coordinating colleges," which then paid all expenses for technical assistance. Technical assistance consisted of campus visitations by members of the ACCTion staff, regional workshops, specialist training, and information dissemination. Three trustees and four presidents comprised the coordinating board, which hired an executive director and small staff, who worked out of a suite at L'Enfant Plaza in Washington, D.C.

"The ACCTion Consortium helped us stay on the cutting edge of a lot of things," recalls Charles King, president of Southwest Virginia Community College, which was a member of the Resource Development component. "It was one of those things where you networked a lot . . . before there was such a thing as networking!"[11]

"We all grew tremendously as a result of the ACCTion workshops," believes Don Garrison. "It had a major impact." One specific outcome was the assistance it rendered to small colleges that previously did not have the wherewithal to submit Title III proposals. Through the Resource Development component, college staff members were given the tools to write Title III proposals.

Beverly Simone, then at Indiana Vocational Technical College, describes how ACCTion benefited both college and individuals.

> Through the ACCTion Consortium, we created a model developmental/remedial program at Ivy Tech and took it out [to other colleges]. We had *no* resources in Indiana. For me personally, it opened up a whole array of knowledge and experience from others that helped us do important things. For instance, I learned to use DACUM [an early assistive technology software program] to create our developmental program.[12]

Mary Ellen Duncan, then with Tri-County Technical College in South Carolina, which housed the Instructional Center, was staff for the project.

> It was the world's best job. We got to work with colleges that wanted to do things. You went to colleges where they wanted to talk about innovation and new programming. We went from place to place. Colleges would show us what they were doing.
>
> We connected people with each other, and we asked them to showcase their programs at workshops. These weren't just huge conferences. You were supposed to *do* something with what you learned. It was a totally different operation. We built a network of people, many of whom were women. ACCTion was a way for people to show what they were doing, to build a network, to move into other positions. Many became presidents.[13]

"ACCTion made a difference to a lot of developing community colleges," believes Connie Sutton-Odems, who was employed in the Student Development Services Center for several years. "It linked these colleges together to learn together and share. Out of that came a Dave Pierce, who, at the time, was president of a small college in Iowa. I can think of many presidents who, because of that humble start, were active on the AACJC board of directors; it became a group of presidents who knew each other. It became a powerful group."[14]

The project was funded two to three years longer than anyone expected initially. Marie is credited with its longevity, and for promoting visibility and understanding about community colleges. It was no small task to free up this kind of money for community colleges, as the Office of Education had a distinct university bias.[15] "Marie Martin was in the pioneering years there, and in that sense conditioned the Office of Education that they ought to pay attention to community colleges." Marie was a "quiet, stable influence."[16]

RAISES FEDERAL PROFILE
FOR COMMUNITY COLLEGES

More than just opening up Title III money for two-year colleges, many acknowledge Marie's key role in increasing visibility of the colleges and their role in higher education. "She was a disciple for us; she spread the word around the country about this new mission."[17] "She was an effective leader in helping to redefine the federal position of community colleges in a couple of administrations."[18] If she made a major contribution,

> it was visibility at the federal level. If there was one person who, when we were trying to get the message out about what we were, it was Marie [who made it happen]. She should be remembered not only for the ACCTion Consortium but because she laid the groundwork for community colleges to take advantage of other federal programs such as FIPSE, Title II, and TRIO. She opened doors for a number of things for community colleges.[19]

Some attribute her accomplishments to the fact that "she was able to see the lay of the land and get things done."[20] Although she was a "quiet, unassuming 'lady,'"[21] she was also "tenacious; she could be sweet or she could be ornery. When she decided what she wanted to do for community colleges, you got out of the way."[22]

Mary Ellen Duncan reports that Marie was deliberate in connecting women with each other. "She didn't have much patience for us being timid, not being bold. She always asked us what we were doing, and what we would be doing next. She was the first person to put the idea into my head of becoming a president. When she sprinkled dust on you, you could do anything."[23]

Additionally, the tremendous success of ACCTion was a shot in the arm for the nascent Association of Community College Trustees. In 1976, it named a leadership award after Marie, acknowledging that her "professional career epitomizes influence on the community college movement at all levels." Maxwell King of Brevard Community College was tapped as the first recipient of the Marie Y. Martin CEO Award. The recognition has been given every year since, and Marie herself presented the award until 1986.

The end of Marie's tenure in Washington is not recorded; she did return to California for her retirement years, working as a search consultant with John Lombardi on presidential searches.[24] Reportedly, she suffered from Alzheimer's disease at the end of her life and died in 1993 at age eighty-two.[25]

Chapter Six

K. Patricia Cross

Influential Writer and Speaker

K. Patricia Cross

No nomination for women of influence in community colleges from this era evokes more consensus than that of K. Patricia Cross. "She really stands so far above the rest—in a class by herself,"[1] as one observer put it.

First appearing on the national scene in the late 1960s through her work with the Educational Testing Service, over the next decades Pat gained legions of admirers in American higher education who took increasing notice of her speeches, articles, and books. Her work resonated with community college administrators and faculty because she focused on understanding the changing nature of the students in American higher education and proposing teaching strategies appropriate to these students.

Here was someone with a masterful grasp of data analysis, affiliated with prestigious institutions, and writing respectfully and clearly about higher education's obligation to help these "new students"—as she labeled them—succeed. Community college administrators and faculty felt supported and understood by Pat Cross, and they gained insights for practice from her work.

Pat describes her childhood as "high socio and low economic."[2] The daughter of physics professor Clarence L. Cross and homemaker Kathryn Dague Cross, Pat grew up in a "loving, close, and supportive family." Born in 1926 and reared in the college town of Normal, Illinois, Pat distinguished herself early as a leader, being elected president both of her senior class and the girl's debate club. She saw her younger sister, Betty, as "really the brains in the family," and reflected that she herself was "more outgoing, a good student but not outstanding."

Her original career goal was to be an architect, but family adherence to frugality dictated that she should start college at home, at Illinois State Normal University, and then transfer to the University of Illinois for study in her chosen field. Although she did not fancy becoming a teacher, a condition of her full-tuition eighty dollar scholarship to Illinois State was that she teach in an Illinois school after graduation. Her plans to transfer to the University of Illinois fell through when she was told that she would have to pay back her first two years' tuition. So she finished at Illinois State and then taught mathematics for a year at Harvard High School in Illinois.

DECIDES TO PURSUE PSYCHOLOGY

Anxious to attend graduate school, Pat enrolled at the University of Illinois to study psychology. Her sister, admitted to the graduate program in economics, joined her as roommate in an off-campus apartment. Although she remembers the psychology program as "absolutely an awful experience," she soon found a niche as a statistician for Raymond B. Cattell, a pioneer in psychological profiling who emphasized the systematic investigation of human personality through the use of multifactor analysis.[3] "There was lots of funding," Pat recalls, "oodles of funding from the federal government for anything to do with psychology."

Although Pat was in demand for her facility with statistics, she was growing increasingly dissatisfied with psychology because of its emphasis on behaviorism. She made an appointment with the dean of women, Miriam Shelden, and explained that she was thinking of switching her doctoral studies from psychology to education. Dean Shelden strongly encouraged her to stay in psychology, advising her that a psychology degree was a more admired academic degree and would place her in better standing for a position such as a college dean.

Remembering Pat's interest in education, Dean Shelden contacted her the following year to report an opening for the Panhellenic dean. Despite the fact that Pat had no sorority experience, she was selected for the position and quickly won over the sorority community. She also gained national renown through being the first in the country to automate sorority rushing with punch cards and IBM machines.

While completing her doctorate, Pat became engaged to a graduate student in physics, and they expected to marry after he completed his service duty during the Korean conflict. Sadly, he died stateside within weeks from what Pat speculates was unprotected exposure to radium during a research project.

Now lacking plans that tied her to Illinois, Pat weighed her career options—whether to pursue an administrative route or to start at the bottom of the faculty ladder as an assistant professor of psychology. Because there was a marked difference in salary, she accepted an appointment as dean of women at Cornell University.

After a year, she was promoted to the newly created position of dean of students. This was an unprecedented appointment for a woman, especially at a school where men outnumbered female students four to one. So noteworthy was the selection that the *New York Times* picked up the story; under the headline "Dean With a Smile,"[4] the article called her "a warm, friendly, out-going person, with a deep and sincere concern for the problems of young people." The story quoted one source saying, "If you awarded the new job on the basis of popularity with the students and staff, she would get it on that basis alone."

After four years at Cornell, Pat became uncomfortable with the increasingly hostile relations between students and college administrations that characterized the student protests of the 1960s. She requested guidance from her thesis adviser, Lee J. Cronbach, at Stanford University. A member of the national advisory committee to the Educational Testing Service (ETS), he suggested that Pat's administrative experience and psychology degree might be attractive to ETS. After a visit to ETS headquarters in Princeton, New Jersey, Pat was "totally taken with them," and, apparently, they with her, so she moved there in 1964.

BEGINS WORKING WITH ETS

Pat's tenure at ETS offered her tremendous flexibility to define a series of creative jobs for herself. For instance, she noticed that ETS offered five testing instruments for higher education. "Why don't we put them all together and offer them as a package?" she suggested. "So, I became director of IRPHE [Institutional Research Program in Higher Education]!"

When Pat began to get campus-based job offers, the president of ETS countered by offering to help arrange a position for her with the prestigious Center for Research and Development in Higher Education at the University of California, Berkeley, where she would split her time between the center and ETS. Center director Leland L. Medsker quickly agreed, offering Pat a choice of assignments. She chose to work on "dissemination and development" rather than research.

All parties agreed that Pat would go to Berkeley for a year in 1966 to write a book about access to higher education. (She "fell in love" with California and never returned to the ETS Princeton headquarters.) Again, she found herself able to define her own work during this "time of great affluence." Pat initiated the *Research Reporter*—an accomplishment of which she was particularly proud—where she interviewed the staff and professors at the center regarding the results of their research and wrote summaries for the *Reporter*. It was through this vehicle that she discovered that one of her "talents really was writing."

Her most ambitious early project at Berkeley was to write *Beyond the Open Door*. It was "a very strange thing to do," she reflects. "We [ETS] were interested in admissions tests, and here I come out with a book that focused on colleges that didn't use them."

PUBLISHES GROUNDBREAKING
WORK ON THE "NEW STUDENT"

Beyond the Open Door, published in 1971, used four major databases available through ETS and the center to look at the characteristics of what Pat labeled "new students." She argued that higher education was not prepared to serve them—those whose personal and educational backgrounds did not mirror students higher education traditionally served prior to open admissions. Rather than concentrating on the "deficiencies" of "new students," she wrote that colleges should concentrate on developing the new range of talents and interests that they bring to higher education and use new methods in order for them to succeed.

Pat proposed that instead of exposing all students to the same curriculum, students should become certified as excellent in one "sphere of excellence" working with a) people, b) things, or c) ideas; and be at least competent in the other two. Such an approach would permit the recognition of excellence across a broad range of talents. When excellence is measured along a single dimension, she wrote, half of the people will always be "below average." She argued that "Human dignity demands the right to be good at something"[5] and quoted John Gardner's eloquent statement in his book, *Excellence: Can We Be Equal and Excellent Too?*

> An excellent plumber is infinitely more admirable than an incompetent philosopher. The society which scorns excellence in plumbing because plumbing is a humble activity and tolerates shoddiness in philosophy because it is an exalted activity will have neither good plumbing nor good philosophy. Neither its pipes [n]or its theories will hold water.[6]

Community college leaders found themselves drawn to these ideas. Pat Cross seemed to speak to the issues with which they were grappling, such as when she wrote in 1968,

> One thing that stands out clearly in this review of research on junior college students is that we possess only the traditional dimensions of education to describe a student who does not fit this tradition. . . . If we posit a single task for all institutions of higher education, the junior college runs the risk of becoming a watered-down version of the four-year college. Such a concept, of course, is not what makes the creation of the junior college one of the most exciting and challenging innovations in higher education in this

century. . . . The great future task for research is to investigate the ways in which junior college students differ in kind or in pattern of abilities rather than in degree from traditional college students.[7]

Her argument that the new student—largely the student population of community colleges at the time—deserved to be educated, and educated well, gave an enormous boost to those in community colleges as it came from someone writing under the auspices of ETS and the Higher Education Center at Berkeley.

When community college presidents and university professors were surveyed in 1979 to determine the "works they felt had influenced the historical development of the community college,"[8] Pat Cross's *Beyond the Open Door* tied for first place among community college presidents and third among university professors of higher education.

Others attribute her importance to the fact that "she was a highly respected outsider 'peeking in' and saying that good things were going on [in community colleges]."[9] "She understood our mission and how we could bring our students up to speed."[10] "Her writing, her academic thinking, her view of community colleges from the university perspective is nearly immeasurable on the field and on those of us who were seeking to ground what we were doing in good academic thought."[11] "She made a significant contribution in development of community college leaders through her publications. She had a point of view of the importance of community college education and had considerable visibility within the movement."[12]

WRITES ADDITIONAL INFLUENTIAL BOOKS

The approach Pat used in writing *Beyond the Open Door*—summarizing research findings on topics of teaching and learning, and concluding with recommendations for practice—characterized her subsequent major works over the next decade: *Accent on Learning* (1976) and *Adults as Learners* (1981).[13]

She wanted her work, she wrote, "to be grounded *in* research rather than grounded *by* research."[14] *Accent on Learning* was largely a call for new teaching techniques, such as mastery learning, to help new students be successful. She devoted particular emphasis on learning styles. Although *Accent on Learning* was her lowest-selling book, Pat sees this work as "one of the shifts toward the new paradigm from teaching to learning. It took my interests in that particular direction."[15]

Pat's next work, *Adults as Learners*, published after she was appointed to the faculty of Harvard's Graduate School of Education, met with huge acclaim. This book spoke favorably and clearly about a hot issue in higher education: who were these adults coming to college, and how might their learning needs best be met?

Once again, this theme spoke to those in community colleges, especially because her affiliation with Harvard did a lot "to legitimate the colleges with her colleagues in the university."[16] "She was a bridge between community colleges and universities in terms of her research and what she talked about. She showed the commonalities to university people."[17]

By the late 1980s, Pat sharpened her focus on successful strategies for teaching and learning. In a standing-room-only speech at the national conference of the American Association for Higher Education in 1986, Pat roused the audience with her keynote address, "Taking Teaching Seriously," in which she urged educators to take the outcomes-assessment movement into the classroom. As a follow-up, Pat published *Classroom Assessment Techniques: A Handbook for College Teachers* with Thomas A. Angelo in 1988.[18]

This workbook cemented her place as the premier leader in the student-centered learning movement. "What was significant is how she put it to the forefront and how she got faculty to understand that they didn't have to be university researchers but could *and needed to* do research in their classrooms."[19] Faculty at hundreds of colleges and universities implemented the ideas on classroom assessment techniques touted in this best-selling book. Subsequently, she coauthored two additional books on classroom-based research.

THE GIFTS OF SYNTHESIZING AND WRITING

Pat's own assessment of her contribution is that she was able to read and synthesize research—particularly from cognitive psychology—for practitioners who didn't have access to that literature.

I was always interested not in research per se, but in the application and use of research. That's why I went to all of this synthesis. I could have collected my own data—because I had the skills to do that—but I was far more interested in what you do with it, and that's what led to these books, all of which are syntheses of other people's work. That is, I have served as a translator, making clear the implications of research for practice.

Generally, it is agreed that Pat had a particular gift for written communication. "She says complex things in a way anyone can understand."[20] "She is always clear and definitive."[21] She possessed a "wonderful blend of creativity, research, and common sense."[22] Virtually no book from this era on community colleges—or on teaching and learning, for that matter—failed to include a citation from her prolific work.

Interestingly, Pat says that she has always "worked terribly hard" at writing. "It takes me an unconscionably long time to write a speech. I can spend a whole morning not putting anything new in, but moving words, changing words." She found it surprising that she became such a sought-after speaker. "I didn't like speaking particularly—it was never on my agenda of things to do."

Although those in community colleges felt that Pat Cross was "speaking to them," as evidenced by the AACJC bestowing its Leadership Award on her in 1990, she also received the highest honors from national organizations representing adult education, student personnel, institutional research, developmental education, independent colleges, instructional administrators, community services, and educational research.

"She was a critical voice in support of community colleges and of our mission, and particularly from the side of education of students, especially underprepared students. She put her stamp on the way we educate our students," says Robert McCabe, who brought Pat to Miami Dade College for a semester in 1987 so that "she could take her theories and see how those theories applied in operation."[23]

In 1988, Pat left Harvard to become the first endowed chair in the School of Education at the University of California, Berkeley, and worked there until her retirement in 1994. She continued to keep active—writing, speaking, and serving on numerous national boards and advisory committees. "I have always been interested in the student," reflects Pat on her body of work. "It probably comes out of my student personnel background. So, you could say, I have always been a champion of the student."

Chapter Seven

Janet E. Lieberman

Serving At-Risk Youth

Janet E. Lieberman

LaGuardia Community College is well recognized as having been a beacon of innovation during the formative years of the contemporary community college movement. Numerous colleges sent staff on fact-finding visits to learn about LaGuardia's learning communities, cooperative education program, and interdisciplinary courses.

One member of the LaGuardia founding faculty played a key role in a number of these programs and was the architect of a landmark innovation: middle college. This groundbreaking and lasting approach to serving at-risk high school students through a partnership between high schools and community colleges was the brainchild of faculty member Janet E. Lieberman.

Janet's arrival on New Year's Eve in 1921 portended a blessed life, according to Jewish tradition. She was the second child of Samuel and Ida Rubensohn, both college educated, with her mother a piano teacher for children in deprived neighborhoods and her father a successful manufacturer of children's clothing. They "lived a very middle-class life"[1] in Flatbush, Brooklyn, a community of aspiring Jewish and Italian families.

Janet attended the Berkeley Institute, an academically oriented girl's school. As her father's career prospered, along with her mother's social ambitions, the family moved to Manhattan and became immersed in the upper echelon of New York Jewish society.

Although neither parent actively encouraged her to continue pursuing education after high school, Janet's respectable academic record earned her admission to Vassar College, which had the advantage of being close to home. Before heading to college, she spent the summer with a family friend in Chicago, where she met a young man from New York. A student at Harvard, Allen Chase came often to Vassar in Janet's freshman year to take her out. They decided to marry when Janet turned eighteen.

AN EARLY MARRIAGE CHANGES HER PLANS

The young couple secured an apartment in Manhattan, and Janet transferred to Barnard College as a day student. Janet felt she should have a useful skill, so she majored in economics with a minor in psychology. She finished her degree requirements in less than three years and in 1945 gave birth to the couple's first child, Gary.

She and her husband became active in the music and cultural scene, and "lived an exciting, interesting cultural life in New York City." But the leisure lifestyle of watching children, playing cards, and golfing did not appeal to her. She recalls, "I knew I didn't want to spend the rest of my life in the park." So, she decided to pursue a master's degree in school psychology at City College, which was tuition free and had a strong program in that discipline. She immersed herself in school psychology courses and found that she loved the field.

By 1954, she was divorced, a mother of two, and had her master's degree. When Gary and her second son, Randy, reached school age, she felt she was in a position to work full-time. Hired by the New York Board of Education as a school psychologist, she evaluated children in Brooklyn and Harlem, determining whether referred students should to go special classes.

After a few years, she was asked by the board to work as a psychologist at what was called a "600 school," for "wayward" pupils—in this case, one hundred troubled girls who posed disciplinary problems in their home schools.

Janet and three others formed the initial school staff, which, each afternoon, would convene to discuss cases with the principal. This experience was formative for Janet, as it taught her how a dedicated faculty could reach a highly at-risk population by creating a nurturing environment. It also opened her eyes to the kinds of lives that many students lived outside the school—children who did not know from where their next meal was coming; children who brought the scars from their chaotic home lives to school with them.

After four years, a disagreement with a new principal caused Janet to look for other work, which she quickly found at Hunter College as a teacher of reading for education majors. By now she realized that a doctorate was required for credibility in the school system. As a single, working mother, it took her ten years to get her PhD in educational psychology from New York University. In 1957, she married Jerry Lieberman, a physician, and received an appointment as assistant professor at Hunter College.

SEEKS A MORE CHALLENGING ENVIRONMENT

Janet spent five years as a reading specialist in the educational clinic at Hunter, but she found that the four-year university setting lacked a feeling of collegiality; there was little sense of ownership or partnership within the school of education. So when Ann Marcus, dean of continuing education of the newly founded LaGuardia Community College in Long Island

City in western Queens, contacted Janet in 1970 about joining the founding faculty as an expert in remediation, she jumped at the chance.

> Everyone thought I was crazy to take the job. Ann Marcus told me what
> they were doing: "It's experimental—you'll be one of seven to eight faculty
> members; you'll be able to help shape the institution, and we want someone
> like you to set up the program." The *challenge* is what appealed to me.
> Status and money it was not. I wanted to have something interesting to do
> and to use my talents in a productive way. This looked like an interesting
> group of people, who were exciting and enthusiastic. They were imbued
> with a sense of mission.

They spent the first eight months planning, "the most exciting eight
months I've ever spent. We *made* a college," says Janet.

The chancellor of the City University of New York had directed La-
Guardia, first, to make this *the* experimental college of CUNY (which
gave the planners a sense of freedom); and, second, to include an intern-
ship/work experience component. The challenge, as the founders saw it,
was to achieve this mission with a population that was going to need a
great deal of remediation and operating within the constraints of being
part of a larger system (CUNY).

Among Janet's first assignments was to visit colleges around the country to gain ideas for how to implement LaGuardia's goal to create "a total
learning experience through which students will gain not only specific
skills and a broad range of knowledge, but also a sense of professional,
financial, and personal responsibility."[2]

Soon after coming to LaGuardia, Janet met with CUNY acting chancellor Timothy Healy, who noted that the significant and persistent New
York City high-school dropout rate limited the potential benefits of
CUNY's new open admissions policy.[3] He asked Janet to design a program to increase LaGuardia's enrollments.

PROPOSES ESTABLISHING AN
ALTERNATIVE HIGH SCHOOL

Influenced by the works of Erik Erikson, Jerome Bruner, and Ernst Boyer,
Janet proposed that LaGuardia establish a high school aimed at high-risk

students that would be located on the campus.[4] Students' high school costs would be assumed by the New York Board of Education, as it was technically an alternative high school. LaGuardia President Joseph Shenker agreed to commit to the planning effort and assigned Janet to head the project.

Knowing that internal funding support was unlikely, the organizers approached a half dozen foundations and government agencies. The proposal struck a chord with E. Alden Dunham, a higher-education program officer for the Carnegie Corporation of New York.

Dunham had served as liaison to the Carnegie Commission on Higher Education, which between 1967 and 1980 commissioned and published some 160 books, each focusing on a timely topic in higher education. He wrote one of the publications, *Colleges of the Forgotten Americans*,[5] in which he identified the community college as the postsecondary institution most likely to collaborate with secondary schools to ensure increased access of minority groups to higher education.

Like Janet, Alden Dunham was optimistic that smaller academic and status distances between community colleges and high schools boded well for "school-college" collaboration. Alison Bernstein of the Ford Foundation believes that, in Janet Lieberman, Dunham found an educational psychologist who thought about adolescent development in a new way. "Instead of pushing them backwards in terms of their age appropriateness, Janet believed you should push them forward, into the college setting. The big breakthrough was to think about kids who were not doing well by traditional measures, and giving them a nontraditional acceleration of their opportunities by putting them in a college setting and treating them like adults."

Dunham visited the college, interviewing CUNY officials, LaGuardia faculty, and New York City high school students. Subsequently, the Carnegie Corporation approved a $95,116 grant that covered planning-year salaries. Dunham also helped create contacts between Janet and officials at FIPSE (Fund for the Improvement of Postsecondary Education in the U.S. Department of Education), which awarded the project funds to support further staff expansion.

The grants permitted Janet's team to flesh out the academic curriculum and funding plans during 1972–1973 and gave the college leverage to obtain approval of the design from the Board of Education, CUNY, and myriad state agencies.

WHAT MAKES A MIDDLE COLLEGE WORK

The school was designed to offer a flexible, multidisciplinary, "relevant" program of studies designed to heighten student interest in education and to permit close articulation between the school's secondary and collegiate components. Placement on a community college campus would help motivate students to increase their aspirations.

The small school size—450 students maximum—ensured personal attention and faculty support. The original plan also included the idea that all students would take a five-year sequence, culminating in a diploma and an associate's degree, although this aspect of the plan was not incorporated until years later with the introduction of the early college concept.

More bold was the decision to recruit underachievers, disaffected high-risk students who had been identified as potential dropouts, rather than targeting students already benefiting from the present high school experience. Other novel aspects of the design included sharing physical space with ongoing college functions; a mandatory cooperative education experience (by then a signature of LaGuardia); small "houses" as the primary group with which students would identify; expanding the role of teachers to include responsibility for the affective development of these high-risk students; and systematic evaluation.

Overcoming numerous funding, bureaucratic, personnel, and political hurdles, Middle College High School (MCHS) at LaGuardia Community College opened in fall 1974. Starting small, the first class enrolled 135 students, whose average reading level was grade 7, mathematics averaging grade 6.6, with nearly three-fourths requiring remediation at the sentence or paragraph writing level. Janet believes, "We made it possible for them to dream about going to college. We showed that this population had promise, and given the right kind of preparation, could make it."[6]

The initial years were marked by turnover of principals, lack of staffing, and an inability to offer cooperative education to all students. But by 1978–79, under successive principals Arthur R. Greenberg and Cecilia (Cece) L. Cullen, the school began to show impressive outcomes. Of the 443 enrolled students—all having been identified as pre-dropouts—the attendance rate was 84 percent, with 85 percent going on to college.[7]

By the mid-1980s, other community colleges began to take notice of these statistics. In 1985, the New York State Legislature funded five replications for New York City, of which one (International High School) was conceived by Janet Lieberman. In 1986, Janet received the first of several grants from the Ford Foundation to replicate the model nationally.

THE MODEL TAKES OFF

Alison Bernstein, then program officer at the Ford Foundation, gave Janet the chance to prove that the middle college model did not rely on one person or one college. "If this is really good," she reasoned, "then someone else should be able to replicate it. At the end of the day, middle college programs must succeed on the basis of local leadership." By 1991, five of the replication sites were considered successful. By 2000, some thirty colleges housed a high school on site, with more in development.

By 2016, some forty-two colleges held membership in the Middle College National Consortium, founded in 1993 by MCHS principal Cece Cunningham. The consortium was named in 2002 by the Bill and Melinda Gates Foundation to coordinate the replication of the "early college" iteration of the middle college concept. The early college model fully integrates grades nine through thirteen, so that students earn a high school diploma and associate's degree within five years, as Janet and the original faculty envisioned back in 1973.

Alfredo de los Santos, former vice chancellor for student and educational development at Maricopa Community College, believes that Janet's greatest contribution was in trying to recruit students to bring them *to* community colleges, especially the black, Puerto Rican, and immigrant white students LaGuardia served. "In the early eighties," he recalls, "we created 2+2+2 programs at Maricopa that continue to this day. The first thing I did after securing board approval of the concept was to get on a plane and fly out to LaGuardia to see Janet."[8]

The then-chancellor of Maricopa, Paul Elsner, sees her as the first person to recognize the possible role that community colleges could play in getting high-risk students out of chaotic high school situations.

We [MCC] have an 80 percent success rate in moving students up to Arizona State University through our ACE [Achieving a College Education] program. All the construction of that program, in its earlier formative years, was primarily because we sent our faculty to see LaGuardia's Middle College. And I went out there and we came back and said, "What a great idea!"

My theory of human development is that most people are underestimated, and that's how the world works. Many people, if given an opportunity with some kind of equitable level playing ground, will do well, and sometimes they will do excellent. And that is what Janet believes in, and that's what middle college represents.[9]

THE POWER OF AN IDEA

Many prominent community college leaders from the early era do not recognize the name of Janet Lieberman, nor were middle colleges pervasive in community colleges by 1990. But her story is included in this collection for several reasons.

First, it exemplifies, as she puts it, "the power of an idea," and the possibilities for bringing it to fruition through tremendous work and focus.

Second, this idea broke so many rules for whom community colleges should be serving, and how they might reach young, at-risk populations, that it has been called "the most renowned example of community college efforts in 'reconnecting youth.'"[10]

Third, Janet's ability to access funds from prestigious foundations and agencies shows how key this was to implementing educational reform during those years.

And finally, Janet is one of many women who never attained a high-ranking position, national prominence, or sought to gain personal recognition for her ideas; yet an important innovation that is still playing out in community colleges today can be traced directly to the assignment she received nearly fifty years ago.

Janet's passion for helping at-risk students sometimes found her at odds with colleagues. "Janet does not suffer fools gladly," opined longtime associate Alison Bernstein. "I liked her spunk," observed Paul Elsner. "She said it like it was." Janet herself admits, "I wasn't that much of a team player. Part of my style is that I never want operational responsibility. I'm very happy engendering ideas, getting them funded, starting them up, and walking away."

In recognition of her efforts that benefited high-risk populations,[11] Janet was awarded the Charles A. Dana Award for Innovation in Higher Education (1989) and a Harold W. McGraw Jr. Prize in Education (2004). After retiring, Janet continued her affiliation with LaGuardia for some years as a consultant and remained active as an innovator, book author, and grant writer.[12]

When asked what drove her accomplishments over the decades, Janet believes that all of her initiatives had the same goal—to make higher education available to disadvantaged youth. "I created pathways both for the students and institutionally, which carried out [Ernst] Boyer's 'seamless web' concept. We needed to make them learners and to make them aware of the possibilities." In short, she wanted "to give underprivileged kids what privileged kids have always had."

Chapter Eight

Connie Dubose Sutton-Odems
National Association Leadership

Connie Dubose Sutton-Odems

When Edmund J. Gleazer, Jr., president of the American Association of Community and Junior Colleges, called Connie Sutton in 1979 to offer her the position of vice president for programs, she was anything but certain of her interest in the position.

Even though it was nearly the 1980s, AACJC remained an all-white enclave, increasingly criticized for the lack of diversity in its governance and management ranks. Was she being asked to assume this position solely by virtue of being a black woman, albeit one who had gained a national reputation for leadership in staff development?

Fifteen years later, when she retired at sixty-two, Connie Sutton-Odems had risen to the position of senior vice president and had served success-fully three presidents of the national association. Credited with keeping AACJC on an even keel under the reign of these presidents of widely divergent personalities and passions, Connie earned the respect of the en-tire community college movement for helping steer the association from "behind the scenes."

Connie's story of her rise from a member of the underclass in the seg-regated South to such an influential position is a lesson in the importance of competency, reputation, and willingness to take career risks.

Born the oldest of five children in 1932 in Tampa, Florida, Connie was the daughter of the Reverend William DuBose Sr., a Baptist minister, and Arimentha DuBose, who, in her early years, taught school. Mrs. DuBose, an organist, had earned a two-year degree from Talladega; Reverend Du-Bose had a two-year degree from Florida A&M.

Ybor City, Florida, the community in which Connie grew up, was populated by Jews, Italians, Cubans, and blacks. Because of that mix of people, Connie learned early on that "all people are alike—it's not your religion, ethnicity, or racial background."[1] But she also learned about prejudice and injustice. She experienced knowing she was black, and that you were not supposed to do certain things. She remembered well the "whites only" and "colored" water fountains.

But her parents taught their children to turn the other cheek, to see the good in people. Her mother thought Connie might be too naive, that she should be more hard-nosed—but "I never succeeded at that!" Growing up, she was taught that she could be whatever she wanted to be.

A SEGREGATED EDUCATION

All of her education was in segregated schools. When she finished high school at age sixteen, she assumed that the next step would be college. Based upon test results, Connie had been offered a scholarship from Hampton Institute in Virginia[2] and also was awarded a scholarship by a local black sorority. At Hampton, she majored in mathematics. "I don't know why . . . they kept saying, 'Girls don't major in math, you're not supposed to be good in math. . . . So it was kind of my 'show-me' thing." Engineering was her long-range goal, but a professor told her that it was not a career field for women.

At Hampton Institute in the early fifties, Connie had her first exposure to white professors. But the winds of the civil rights movement were in the air, and Hampton hired its first black president while she was a student. Hampton also began to hire black faculty, which she claims made a marked difference in her outlook on life. And Hampton had a number of student-exchange programs with predominantly white institutions.

She found herself drawn to interracial groups, which she attributes to her background growing up with people from different ethnic groups. And her father was in the Ministerial Alliance, which exposed the family to a variety of religions.

Connie decided to teach mathematics at the high school level, even though one of her advisers told her that that would be a problem because she was just twenty and some of her students would be seventeen and eighteen. After graduating from Hampton in 1953, she returned to Florida for a teaching job in Kissimmee. There she met her future husband, Milton Sutton.

The school administration assumed that Connie's background would be useful in interpreting test results, so she was asked to chair a testing committee. Soon, she realized that she was interpreting tests without understanding the psychology behind them. As this was during the *Sputnik* era— when the federal government was looking for counselors to direct people into math and science careers—the school principal encouraged her to get her master's degree, and she received a scholarship through the National Defense Education Act to enroll in Atlanta University's two-year program in education with an emphasis on counseling. She completed her degree in two summers and a year by taking a leave of absence from her teaching job.

SOON MOVES INTO COMMUNITY COLLEGE WORK

By the time she completed graduate school in 1964, her marriage was dissolving, and she realized she was going to be a career person. She was offered a job in Hollywood, Florida, at Attucks High (a black school) as a counselor, which she accepted. Soon she found herself at a College Board conference for counselors in Miami focused on getting minority students into community colleges. Peter Masiko, then president of Dade County Junior College, as it was called then, was in attendance and "as fortune would have it," they sat together. They began chatting, and Masiko said they were looking to hire minorities.

Florida's community colleges had been founded as segregated schools, which Masiko was determined to change at Miami Dade. Under him, the campus designated for blacks (at a high school) was closed down, and these students were integrated into the other campuses. Connie accepted his offer to go to Miami Dade. She was the first black counselor, and one of only a few black faculty members.

> Those were interesting years for me. You get thrust into a leadership role when you are part of a minority, and you are working with both black and white students to achieve equality. Black students, to get them to understand that you are entitled to this, that you deserve this. . . . Civil rights was pretty hot. Students were more and more looking into what their "rights" were. So there was a lot of activism going on on campus. In the midst of all this, I'm a counselor. I'm supposed to be able to mediate.

During those years, Connie began to see the importance of professional development for faculty and staff. The Florida legislature had ruled that 3 percent of college budgets had to be set aside for staff development, and Miami Dade capitalized on this by establishing a special office charged with developing programming for the college.

Thus, Connie entered into a career focus that established her initial reputation as a staff development "expert." She served as the office's assistant director; people came from around the country to learn about the program; Miami Dade staff went to other colleges to help set up their programs. She stayed in this position for several years.

Around this time Florida declared that each college needed an office of equal access/equal opportunity. Again, President Masiko asked her to coordinate a college-wide steering committee that would sponsor training on each campus and coordinate campus documentation of goals and outcomes in achieving student and faculty diversity. In this position, she conducted many workshops on faculty attitudes; she saw equal access as an opportunity for professional development.

STARTS TO BE RECOGNIZED NATIONALLY

Miami Dade sent a group of staff, including Connie, to a workshop sponsored by the National Training Laboratories (NTL) Institute in Bethel, Maine, to learn how to be group facilitators/leaders.[3] Connie emerged from the workshop as a "different kind of leader" and was tapped by NTL to be part of its yearlong leadership internship program. This triggered the need for her to decide between taking a leave to get her doctorate, which she had been contemplating, or participating in the NTL internship.

Thinking that she could always get her doctorate later and that Miami Dade would give equivalent professional credit toward promotion for the internship, she chose the latter.

"Deciding to take the internship was the best decision I made in my life," says Connie. Most NTL Institute interns were from business and government, so it exposed her to other ways of being a professional. She started doing consulting workshops with NTL with business and industry and stayed active with NTL during the seventies and early eighties.

In 1975, the center director for the Student Development Component of the ACCTion Consortium,[4] Lee Betts, called; he wanted her to head the staff development component, which was headquartered at Hesston College in Kansas. "Your name keeps coming up," he told her, "and we need you to be a part of this." To accept his offer would mean taking another leave from Miami Dade; Pete Masiko again agreed to give her a leave without pay, and if it did not work out, allow her to return to her old job.

She moved to Kansas and stayed until fall 1978. Soon, the executive director of the ACCTion Consortium asked Connie to go to Washington, D.C., to head up staff development, and she agreed. Within a year's time, AACJC president Edmund Gleazer called her to say that they had an opening for a vice presidency, and "your name keeps coming up." The job was vice president for programs, one of five vice presidential jobs at AACJC at the time. Gleazer said that her greatest supporter was Pete Masiko, who, at the time, was chair of the AACJC board.

Learning that Masiko was promoting Connie for the position upset her—why, she wondered, would he be so supportive of her taking this job and not coming back to Miami Dade? Masiko reassured her that it was because he thought she was the right person for the job, and that after her exposure to programs with a nationwide scope, she could never be happy at Miami Dade again.

BEGINS HER AFFILIATION WITH AACJC

So she agreed to have lunch with Edmund Gleazer and Roger Yarrington, Gleazer's second in command, and she perceived that they were clearly "checking her out." Later, she went to Detroit for the ACCT convention and, while having a drink with David Pierce (an old friend from the ACCTion Consortium days), someone came up to tell her that she had an important phone call from Gleazer. She returned the call in the morning, and he offered her the job. Hesitant to say yes, she took a couple of days and talked to some people whom she trusted. Their response was, "What do you have to lose?"

Despite being anxious about taking such a major, highly visible assignment, she started at AACJC in January 1980. In retrospect, she saw herself as a "twofer—a woman and black. They never had a minority or female vice presidency before. I was it. I had a lot of well-wishers across the country, especially from presidents whose campuses I had been on."

> I knew that one of the reasons I was hired was because the association was under pressure to have more minorities. The Black Caucus—a group of black presidents—was at a convention in Hawaii, in 1978, and caused a real big thing on the floor of the business meeting of the convention about the lack of minority staff. And so the board felt that pressure. The association did not have a good record of bringing in minority people.
>
> But I also knew that I wouldn't have gotten where I was without being competent. I had a successful track record and knew I could carry my weight, and somebody else's, too. So how I saw myself in that role made a difference, too. I didn't go in feeling that I was the "token" black. I went in feeling that I was the vice president who was very competent for the position, who happened to be black, and that was a plus.

Her responsibilities included organizing the workshops for the President's Academy (dedicated to renewal and recognition of CEOs), coordinating the work of various task forces and commissions, and, most importantly, heading up the annual national convention. In part, because of Connie's leadership,[5] the convention became the largest gathering in higher education. Along with the convention staff, she involved herself in site inspections, oversaw the contract, and developed the program—which was a year-round effort. And as board secretary to the association, her duty was to maintain board records, elections, minutes, and archives.

> All of this was stretching me. I was growing and loving it. I was traveling a lot. It was important to me that staff could be trusted. I didn't like to micromanage. I was impatient with people who needed day-to-day maintenance. I try to get people trained and then turn it over. My goal was to do less and less of that. But I wanted to be part of the crunch times along with my staff. I got my hands dirty. They appreciated that.

Edmund Gleazer retired from AACJC in 1981. He had been very supportive of Connie and her work and felt pride and ownership in having hired her. "She was a visible administrator," says Gleazer. "This was important because she was a woman and a minority at a time when AACJC was demonstrating its more comprehensive reach."

LEADERSHIP TRANSITION AT AACJC

Dale Parnell was hired as the new president, coming in with a mandate from his board to diversify the profile of the AACJC leadership; he moved quickly to change the association's top management, including naming a woman to head communications. Gleazer viewed the role of the colleges as a catalyst for community renewal; Parnell, who came out of a vocational-occupational background, envisioned the colleges partnering with business and industry to "put America back to work."[6] Consequently, the people he began to bring in for program development were skilled in workforce and economic development.

Connie believes that what she was able to contribute to Parnell's tenure was her professionalism. "He could trust me to carry his thoughts. I knew what he meant. I was a confidante. We talked about issues relating to the board, AACJC, work-related concerns. It was a personal as well as a professional relationship."

Dale Parnell credits Connie with doing a great deal

> to bring the African American community along in their view of community colleges. She worked hard behind the scenes, pushing me, to bring

women and minorities into positions of leadership. She made sure women and minorities were always included in activities of the President's Academy, whose participants were sitting and newly appointed presidents. In our meetings, she was always looking out for whether there were women and minorities on the councils. And [she saw to it that] there was always a woman in line for the chairmanship.[7]

In turn, Connie believes that Dale Parnell was committed to affirmative action, "in his heart," and recalls many very open conversations with him about this issue.

During the 1980s and early 1990s, AACJC was considered the "primary show in town."[8] Its annual convention was considered a "must attend" by community college presidents. The conference theme often set the national agenda for community colleges. Many credit Connie with much of the success of the convention in those years.

"In developing AACC programs, she was a very good guide in developing sessions, the types of people to use, how to engage an audience. She was always a good bellwether for topics that were timely," recalls Richard Alfred, who headed the Consortium for Community College Development at the University of Michigan.[9] Notes Richard Ernst, then president of Northern Virginia Community College, "she brought together the leadership of the day to those meetings, including leaders from outside community colleges. She knew them all."[10]

DIVERSIFIES AACJC COMMISSIONS AND PANELS

Equally important were the AACJC special-focus councils and task forces. These groups, such as the Building Communities, Put America Back to Work, and the Futures commissions, were looked to for guidance and direction for the evolving movement. Although the president and his board identified the topics for study, Connie is said to have put together many of the blue-ribbon panels, always keeping in mind the need for broad representation. One of her greatest strengths was her "knowing people nationally, so that the best talent could be drawn into positions of leadership in the association."[11]

Connie was "maybe the leading black female in America in community colleges for several years. [She was] a real backbone of the AACJC organization during those years, organizing the conventions, bringing leadership together. [She was] always focused on issues," recalls Johnas (Jeff) Hockaday.[12] Over time, those working with her knew that, while not speaking for Dale Parnell, he would back her. This "allowed Dale to write, to travel. You couldn't do that if your shop was not in good hands. In other words, she served as the inside president," notes Nolen Ellison, then president of Cuyahoga Community College.[13]

Connie's presence in front of and behind the scenes was enormously important to blacks and other minorities in the field. Alfredo de los Santos of Maricopa Community College perceived that she was "very influential within inner circles of AACC decision making, and represented us well. She was a quiet, calming influence in an era of confrontation and an era of transition."[14]

Nolen Ellison saw Connie performing the critical job of ensuring minority representation on panels, "to keep all minority groups comfortable."[15] Texas legislator Wilhelmina Delco, who served on the Commission on Minority Concerns, recalls that Connie was "very important to what we were doing."[16]

Belle Wheelan said Connie was "the only minority in a leadership position in AACJC that I knew about. Otherwise—if you didn't have such a person—there would be no voice at the operational level for any of the programming. She was responsible for ensuring diversity in panels and presenters at the national conference."[17] To Nolen Ellison, "her very presence made it clear that Dale Parnell had absolute confidence in qualified blacks."[18] He, like many others, stressed that her presence was not merely symbolic.

When told that others acknowledged her work in this regard, Connie responded, "Oh, they used to probably get tired of me saying that . . . 'make sure this committee is balanced, gender-wise, and ethnicity-wise.' That was very important." As far as looking for new talent, Connie says, "The Carolyn Williamses, the Walter Bumphuses, the Jackie Belchers . . . people who I saw as deans, that when things came up, they should be included. I was doing this all along. I saw this as professional development."

Not expecting to marry again, Connie found personal happiness as she neared retirement when she met Linn Odems, a retired military officer. A widower, Odems worked for the government in aeronautical services, and had one son and three daughters. They married in 1984 and shared family and faith for nineteen years until his death in 2001.

As Dale Parnell neared the time for his planned retirement after ten years, Connie was "sad to see him go but knew also that it was time for him to go. And I was struck with the fact, 'Gee, all these people coming and going, and I'm still here!'"

NAMED SENIOR VICE PRESIDENT

Connie had known the AACJC president-designee David Pierce for many years and knew that he would bring a different set of skills and approaches, especially in fiscal management. AACJC was experiencing fiscal problems as membership fees rose and federal and foundation funds were not keeping up with association activities.

With a mandate from the board to make the association solvent, upon his arrival in 1992, Dave Pierce reorganized the management structure, making all the vice presidents into directors. Connie was named senior vice president and continued in this role until her retirement in 1994.

From interviews with many people about Connie Sutton-Odems' role during these years from 1980 to 1994, certain phrases keep coming up: "A very visible administrator"[19]; "Quiet individual who got things done"[20]; "The glue that held AACJC together"[21]; "Great organization and management skills."[22]

Clearly, Connie was a strong, steady influence who, as a competent and influential person within AACJC, gave a huge boost to people of color in the field in need of that kind of leadership. She was always on the lookout for new leaders, and she gave them chances to shine in the national spotlight. By virtue of AACJC's preeminence on the national scene during that era, anyone who had a leadership position with the association at that time had the potential to be influential. And clearly Connie Sutton-Odems was that.

> I was the continuity in the executive staff at AACJC for fifteen years, even though the organization was in transition with leadership, programs, and direction. . . . That was because I was there all that time, I could connect the past to the present to the future. I was definitely the backbone, in terms of behind-the-scenes person, that made things happen.

Chapter Nine

Mildred Bulpitt and Carolyn Desjardins

Developing Women Leaders

Two women, each contributing her unique talents to a single purpose, are widely credited with changing the face of leadership in community colleges.[1] Through the National Institute for Leadership Development, Mildred Bulpitt and Carolyn Desjardins paved the way for hundreds of women to move up through the leadership ranks in community colleges. How two women—who themselves never expected to go to college after finishing high school—came to achieve such a feat is a remarkable story.

Born in 1926 to Tom John Bulpitt, a nurseryman, and Mildred Bernice Bulpitt, a housewife, Mildred went to work as an accounting clerk for Pitney

Mildred Bulpitt

Bowes in Stamford, Connecticut, after high school. Soon realizing that the job offered little opportunity for promotion, she went back to a favorite history teacher to ask how to get to college. The teacher took her to the principal's office and, Mildred recalls, "for the first time, I saw that I had graduated sixteenth out of a class of 560."[2] With the support of her financially strapped parents, she moved to Storrs to attend the University of Connecticut and took a job on campus to help pay the $127 per semester fee.

After completing a baccalaureate in English in 1948, Mildred applied to graduate programs and chose Washington State College in Pullman, as it offered her a $900 teaching assistantship. The chair of the English department introduced her to a professor in the School of Education named Marty Martorana, who was teaching a new course on junior college education, which Mildred found "fascinating."

GETS FIRST COMMUNITY COLLEGE JOB

Upon completing her master's in 1950, a tight job market brought about by the deployment of troops for the Korean War led Mildred to take secretarial and clerical positions for the next several years in Pullman and California. In 1952, she landed a job teaching at Northern Wyoming Community College. Typically for that era, the college operated out of an old building, and teachers wore more than one hat. Mildred taught twenty-two different courses in the first year, in English, drama, and journalism, besides acting as adviser to the yearbook and newspaper staffs.

In 1955, Mildred moved to Phoenix College in Arizona, then a part of the high school system, where she taught English, U.S. history, and geography. By 1960, she was asked to head the Evening College, and she was named dean the following year.[3] She quickly established a reputation for innovation, particularly in developing partnerships through community outreach.

Some of her contributions included television courses starting as early as 1961, on-base instruction for Air Force personnel, and training for fire and safety personnel for local governments, beginning in 1962. "She was one of the first to look at adult learners, to understand the diversity of the population that was out there."[4] Simultaneously, she was working toward her doctorate in educational administration and supervision from Arizona State University, which she received in 1970.[5]

WOMEN FIND THEIR PLACE AT THE AACJC TABLE

In 1973, Mildred attended a workshop in California organized by Eileen Rossi from City College of San Francisco and Janice Branstrom from Lane Community College in Oregon. They had received federal funding to hold a four-week leadership development program for women in community colleges, modeled after one they had attended for university women. Mildred recalls:

> When the conference got toward the end, we couldn't bear the thought that it would just stop. We decided we would create something. I had experience setting up the first council for AACJC (for evening programs), so I made some calls . . . and was told you had to have viable national membership and goals. . . . I agreed to be vice chair for council development and membership, and since Eileen had hosted the workshop, she became the first national chairperson. We went for council membership by spring. It started with twenty-one states and two hundred-plus members. So they couldn't refuse us.

Thus was born the American Association of Women in Community and Junior Colleges (AAWCJC),[6] a group that Edmund Gleazer, then president of AACJC, characterized as "burrs under the saddle blanket,"[7] which worked "assertively" to give visibility to the women involved professionally in community colleges. Quickly, AAWCJC became "the national voice for women in community colleges."[8]

In 1975, Mildred was elected national chairperson of the council. Importantly, the organization took advantage of the AACJC's practice of allowing councils to nominate candidates to stand for election to the AACJC board and then working to get them elected. Thus, women such as Kay McClenny and Beverly Simone won seats on the board, even though they were not sitting presidents.

Mildred recalls that although the group prospered and gained members, it lacked a focus until a meeting in 1979, when Carol Eliason of AACJC presented the council with figures about the number of presidencies opening up over the coming ten-year period. The group acknowledged that although women held third-level positions such as associate deans, chairpersons, and directors, few were at the dean's level, particularly as deans of instruction, the most common path to the presidency. "So we finally decided to get serious and do something for women and get them prepared to take them from where they were, and get them ready to move up."[9]

Of those active in AACWJC in those years, Mildred is recognized as "helping AAWCJC become better organized and taking on women's issues as part of our policy agenda."[10] "What Mildred was doing was saying 'How do we raise the visibility of women and get them into [key] positions?'"[11] Mildred Bulpitt was in a propitious position to move this notion forward, as she was then both national chairperson of the AAWCJC and Maricopa Community College's liaison to the League for Innovation.

Coincidentally, Terry O'Banion, the league's executive director, had been urging the National Identification Project of the American Council on Education that "something was needed just for women in community colleges."[12] At that time, fewer than fifty females were U.S. community and junior college presidents.[13] A meeting was called that included Mildred, among others. The assembled group wrote a preliminary proposal to FIPSE (Fund for the Improvement of Postsecondary Education) titled "Leaders for the '80s."

FIPSE FUNDS A LEADERSHIP INSTITUTE
FOR COMMUNITY COLLEGE WOMEN

FIPSE requested a full proposal, and at the 1980 AACJC annual conference, active AAWCJC members, including Betty Steege, Jane Merritt, Mildred Bulpitt, Marge Blaha, and Joyce Elsner, wrote most of the final proposal, again with assistance from Terry O'Banion. That summer, they received word that FIPSE would fund the project at $50,000 per year for three years; the league would serve as the fiscal agent, and Maricopa would contribute office space and Mildred's time as project director.

Anxious to begin operations before funding became available in October, Mildred received permission to hire a half-time coordinator from within the district. When the position was posted, Mildred recalls:

> I didn't know Carolyn Desjardins well, although I had served on a couple of committees with her and heard a lot of fine things about her women's pro-

gram at Mesa College. So I called her and said, "I really think you should apply." She said, "Oh, I couldn't do that." "Well, why not?" "Because I have this program, I've got these courses I teach, the Women's Program, the Women's Center . . ." And I said, "If you can't leave it, then what have you created?" She paused for a few minutes, then said, "Well, I'll think about it."

Carolyn did apply and was selected over three other applicants. Her selection had a profound impact on the future of the Leaders for the '80s project, as Carolyn became "the number-one leader as far as leadership for women [in community colleges]."[14]

As with Mildred, Carolyn's rise to national prominence was not preordained by the circumstances of her early years. Born Carolyn Dooley in northern Idaho in 1930, her father, Roy, was a laborer; her mother, Nellie, a housewife. From the beginning, she loved school and was highly athletic. But although she finished high school with top honors, she had no money to go to college. Instead, she worked as county treasurer and married Stanley Desjardins, her high school sweetheart, when she was twenty.

When Stanley returned from a tour of duty in Korea, Carolyn urged him to take a path other than sawmill operator and instead use the GI Bill to go

Carolyn Desjardins

to college. The family, now including daughters Sandra and Joni, moved to Moscow so Stanley could attend the University of Idaho. Although Carolyn hoped for more children, a hysterectomy at age twenty-seven precluded that possibility. Upon graduation, her husband was offered a job in Brigham City, Utah.

GRIEF LEADS TO DESIRE FOR EDUCATION

Carolyn's comfortable world was shattered with the death of daughter Joni when she was in fifth grade. "She was given over to despair," recalls her daughter Sandra (Sandy).[15] Believing the only way out of her depression was to go to college, she suggested to her husband that she could drive to Weber State in Ogden—the closest college location, thirty minutes away. Stanley refused her request.

Not easily discouraged, Carolyn announced a year later that she *would* be driving to Weber State with her friend Lois, whose husband had recently died. Sandy recalls,

> Dad was not happy about it, but submitted to it. So she would see me off to school each day, then drive with Lois to Ogden. We would do our homework together in the evenings.[16]

At age thirty-nine, Carolyn received her bachelor's degree in counseling/ psychology. She had been one of only two reentry women on the campus. Her husband's work next took him to Phoenix, and once there, Carolyn immediately registered at Arizona State University in the master's in counseling program. By 1978, she also had earned her PhD in counseling. After starting college at thirty-four, Carolyn had completed three degrees within nine years.

Her first job was filling in for a year as associate dean of students at Phoenix College. She loved working with college students and took charge of several student clubs. By the end of the year, she had "fallen in love with community colleges but wanted to do more counseling."[17]

Carolyn secured a counseling position at Mesa College in the Maricopa system, later moving to counseling chair, and then starting a Reentry for

Women program. "She loved that job so much," recalls her daughter Sandy. "She worked well with everyone. She felt it was where it was at for her. Her attention was always on the future of community colleges—these were places where women could excel, especially in leadership. There would be places open for women."

Around 1975, Stanley quit his job without telling his family, and, eventually, the marriage was dissolved. Although her mother went through years of pain over this, daughter Sandy believes that "it was a gift in her life because she never would have grown in the ways that she did if she and my father had stayed together. She poured herself into friends, activities, and to realizing her potential. She blossomed."

JOINS BULPITT IN RUNNING LEADERS FOR THE '80S

After Carolyn accepted the grant-funded position in Leaders for the '80s, she and Mildred began crisscrossing the country offering workshops for women interested in upward mobility within community colleges. The project was based on their belief that women would not begin to penetrate the rank of president until a sufficient number were moving along in the pipeline toward that position.

Using a format of weeklong workshops (one each year in Phoenix, two others in league colleges around the country), they selected speakers on topics such as interview skills, strategic planning, and budgeting, which the participants "had less exposure to."[18] They also required that participants be recommended by their presidents—which had the effect of identifying internally which women were interested in moving up in administration—and that they choose a project to complete within the year under the guidance of a mentor. "Most of these women had never been in this kind of supportive relationship before," notes Mildred.

The workshops did more than strengthen these future leaders' skill sets. For the first time, women with ambitions for upward mobility were getting to know each other and to form what they saw as a corollary to the Old Boys Network. "It was women helping women for the first time."[19] Employing the then-popular consciousness-raising techniques, Carolyn taught women how to value themselves, manage rejection, and look for competencies in a different way than just the résumé.[20] The project was "important in developing a network of women to help each other."[21]

Together, Mildred and Carolyn offered these Leaders for the '80s workshops from 1981 to 1989. At one point, they calculated that they had spent the equivalent of six months in hotel rooms together. And as the project gained visibility and momentum, "institutions were looking for women who were working for them and saying, 'Who has potential?' Even if you only sent two of the five women you had identified as interested in NILD [National Institute for Leadership Development], it began to increase your consciousness about the quality of the women on your staff."[22]

When the FIPSE grant was renewed for 1982–85, the project title changed to National Institute for Leadership Development (NILD). Long-serving college president Constance Carroll believes that the power of the "Leaders" initiative was its grounding in three assumptions:

> That discrimination against women at all levels was alive and well; that women were held to a different standard of achievement than men; and that in order to achieve the highest leadership levels, women needed separate training, strategies, and assistance unique to their situation. All these issues were forthrightly addressed in the Leaders for the '80s program.[23]

COMPLEMENTARY SKILLS AND STRENGTHS

All agree that Mildred and Carolyn complemented each other's strengths and styles. Carolyn "was the counselor, the people-person; Mildred was the conceptualizer."[24] Mildred "gets more credit for the conceptual building blocks that Carolyn then put in place. Mildred was "Type A—better at organizing."[25]

Carolyn, with her counseling background, was the person with feeling and emotion."[26] Carolyn "had the energy, the 'hug factor.' Mildred was more distant and professional, while Carolyn was more bubbly, always doing counseling and therapy. They worked well together, not letting individual egos get in the way. Mildred was important because she trained Carolyn to 'think nationally' and to 'work nationally.' It was a joint merging of energy and the vision to move women up in administration nationwide."[27]

Mildred agreed with that assessment. "Carolyn and I were good to-gether. I had a lot of the contacts that were necessary, from my league membership. I could call all these people at the colleges and say, 'Hey, send us people.' As years went on, Carolyn got to know them, too."

As Mildred moved into phased retirement at Maricopa, Carolyn be-came the driving force behind NILD and, for many, the person recognized for the gains achieved by women who had been NILD participants. By all accounts, Carolyn Desjardins was a truly remarkable woman. Many describe her as "charismatic," "in such a way that she magically drew people to her."[28]

"Carolyn had a way of making all kinds of people—primarily women—feel that they were her very best friend. There are probably a hundred women walking around in the community colleges thinking they were Carolyn's best friend," muses Marie Pepicello Kane.[29] But she also could be tough-minded. "She was not afraid to battle and say, 'This is important.'"[30] "She did wonderful things for women, sometimes by the weight of her will."[31]

In the midst of her deep involvement with NILD, Carolyn took time off in 1985 for a postdoctoral fellowship at Harvard's Graduate School of Education. Among her accomplishments from that experience was coauthoring *The Leading Edge: Competencies for Community College Leadership in the New Millennium.*[32]

Carolyn's influence went beyond the women whose careers she sought to enhance. She, along with others, recognized that Maricopa Community College's chancellor Paul Elsner was instrumental in the success of these efforts, as he supported the project financially and organizationally from its inception. Internally, "Paul set the expectation that women who wanted to move up needed to go through NILD."[33]

But Paul Elsner believes that Carolyn was a very expansive thinker, who, through research, had developed advanced theories about organizations.

If I had effectiveness at Maricopa [as chancellor], it was owing more to Carolyn Desjardins than any other single individual. I was operating like the old guys used to operate—control, watch out over the horizon. She be-lieved that this was missing the point. Control and hierarchy are not where it's at. You need a theory of empowerment, one that develops competencies and capacity in others. You have to have some tolerance and ambiguity in an organization. You need to look at uncertainties and build upon those as opportunities. If your group seems to be out of control, maybe it's when they're at their most productive.[34]

PROJECT RESULTS IN INCREASE
IN FEMALE PRESIDENTS

By the early 1990s, more than 150 women had achieved community college presidencies.[35] In an interview in 1996, Carolyn reported that, of 3,000 graduates of NILD programs, 82 had gone on to become college and university presidents, with another 953 ready to make similar moves based on their experience and other factors.[36]

But at the top of her game, in 1994, Carolyn learned that she had colorectal cancer. According to her daughter Sandy, she "refused to believe" her doctors' prediction that she had six months to live. Indeed, she lived another three and a half years. During that time, she continued to offer and build NILD programming and was able to attend the AACC convention in which she was presented with its prestigious Leadership Award.

She also became active in designing and offering gender-training workshops around the country, believing that "it was important for people to understand that we are more alike than we know."[37] Her death at age sixty-seven was marked by an outpouring of tributes from those she had touched around the country.

Before her retirement, Mildred Bulpitt was named Woman of the Decade in 1983 by the Association for Women in Community and Junior Colleges for her vision for and dedication to the status of women in community colleges. Into her late seventies, Mildred stayed close to NILD by providing informal advice to and brainstorming with its president, Carrole Wolin, and by dropping by the workshops when they were held in Phoenix. She even launched a fund-raising effort to support NILD programs. Mildred died in 2015.

The National Institute for Leadership Development, now called the AAWCC Leaders Institute, continues today in the tradition of Bulpitt and Desjardins. The Leaders Institute still uses many of the aspects Carolyn and Mildred introduced more than twenty-five years ago: the format, most of the topics, inclusion of a pragmatic project pertinent to the participant's college, and the creation of a long-lasting relationship with a mentor. But more importantly, women who aspire to grow as professionals continue to see the Leaders Institute as a nurturing forum to test their interest in and aptitude for leadership positions in community colleges.

Chapter Ten

Suanne Davis Roueche

Celebrating Teaching Excellence

Suanne Davis Roueche

Mention of the name Suanne Roueche often elicits the reaction, "I've never been able to separate Suanne's contributions from John's." Married to one of the most visible university leaders in the community college movement over many decades, Suanne did not seek to carve out an identity apart from that of her husband, John E. Roueche, who long served as professor and director of the Community College Leadership Program at The University of Texas at Austin.

But upon closer examination, one discovers a woman who found her way into community college education and who had the good fortune to team up with a person she believes brought out the best of her talents. Although a partner with John in writing numerous books, articles, and presentations, she gained individual credit for her work in developmental education and for building the National Institute for Staff and Organizational Development (NISOD) into a premier national resource for community college faculty and administrators.

Suanne was born a fifth-generation Texan in 1942. Her father, Raymond Louis Davis, attended Hill County Junior College, and her mother, Edna Sue Leatherwood, earned a degree in business administration from North Texas State Teachers College. As her father was in the service and her mother wished to be with him until he left for overseas duty, shortly after her birth Suanne was left in the care of her maternal grandparents in a small central Texas town, Itasca.

Even after her mother's return, Suanne continued to live primarily with her grandparents until she celebrated her sixth birthday and returned to Dallas to join her parents and enroll in first grade. However, her grandparents remained enormous forces and role models in her life as she returned to live with them every summer until she graduated high school.

Her grandmother, Tommie Allen Leatherwood, had a profound impact on Suanne. "Miss Tommie," who had a master's degree in mathematics, "ran the town"—through her involvement in elections, church activities, and numerous social functions. By getting Suanne involved in all of her civic and social activities, and treating her as an adult, "she simply led me to believe that I was capable of doing and being anything I wanted."[1]

FROM TEACHING IN HIGH SCHOOL
TO COMMUNITY COLLEGE

After earning a bachelor's degree in English from North Texas State University (NTSU) in 1964, Suanne began teaching high school English. She married her high school sweetheart and had a daughter, Robin Sue. Suanne completed her master's in English at NTSU in 1967 while continuing to teach senior English.

Yet she "didn't feel right" in the high school setting. Suanne had begun talking with friends who were teaching at the relatively new community college (El Centro College, the first of seven colleges to be built as campuses of the Dallas County Community College District) in the heart of downtown Dallas, and the idea of teaching there intrigued her. She knew by reputation the people who had thrown their support behind the new district, and it seemed to be just the challenge she was looking for.

So she walked into El Centro College's employment offices in 1966 and asked, "Do you have any openings? I want to teach here." She was told that the English department had no openings but the division of guided studies had a vacancy. Suanne quickly accepted the proffered opportunity to teach writing to students considered academically at-risk, seriously in need of completing remedial work prior to enrolling in regular English courses.

In addition to teaching remedial English to daytime students, Suanne agreed to teach Shakespeare to more traditional students in the evening. A year into that schedule, she found herself far more intrigued with the basic writing students, who, among others, included welfare mothers, adults attempting to enter training programs, newly released county jail inmates, and recent high school graduates who could not pass the English sections of the basic skills assessment tests.

> I found these students to be more engaging. . . .When somebody really needs you to be successful in an unfamiliar situation . . . *maybe* you can do something . . . it was a compelling challenge. I found I was really good with [these students]. It's the most fun I'd ever had. The others were going to make it without you. But these students just might well make it *because* of you.

Suanne was fortunate to be in a district that supported remedial instruction, which was more frequently being referred to as "developmental" education. El Centro's president, Don Rippey, had been approached by the movers and shakers of Dallas to ensure that this new college would serve all of Dallas, especially that it would address the growing literacy problem. "There was a lot of support for the college saying to students, 'If you want to come here, we will put you into programs that will really help you make it to where you want and need to go.'"

CONSIDERS ATTENDING GRADUATE SCHOOL

In 1972, John Roueche was invited to El Centro College as its May commencement speaker. While touring the campus, he was impressed by Suanne's rounding up her wayward developmental English students from the game rooms in the college basement and putting them on elevators to go to class. He suggested that should she ever want to attend graduate school, specifically the Community College Leadership Program (CCLP) at The University of Texas at Austin (UT), he could offer her scholarship assistance.

Suanne replied that she was never going to graduate school again, that she was happy where she was. "Okay," John replied, "but let me know if you change your mind."

Just one year later, she did just that when she was passed over for an administrative position and was told that she needed a doctorate to be considered seriously for a role outside the classroom. She called John the next day to take him up on his offer of financial support for graduate work. As she was divorcing at the time, she left her daughter in her mother's care while she took a leave of absence from El Centro College with plans to move to Austin for only one year of required on-campus coursework.

After just six months at UT, she reported to her department chair at El Centro that she would not be returning to her old position or to the college—it was, in fact, going to be very difficult to go home again. The role of classroom teacher "was not mine any longer. I felt that new perspectives and experiences were drawing me in other directions."

Suanne envisioned herself conducting public policy research and wrote her dissertation on affirmative action policies and initiatives. She and John married shortly after she completed her doctorate in 1976. They combined families to raise John's son, Jay, and Suanne's daughter as much like brother and sister as possible.

DEEPENS HER FOCUS ON LITERACY
AND DEVELOPMENTAL EDUCATION

Suanne and John's first coauthored book, *Developmental Education: A Primer for Program Development and Evaluation*, appeared in 1977.

After a year of directing the Community College Internship Program—an academic service arm of the CCLP—Suanne served as director of a three-year literacy development project, funded by the National Institute of Education. Her experience as a developmental English instructor served her well, as she directed multidisciplinary teams observing classroom instruction, student performance, and success levels in literacy development initiatives, programs, and classes in selected Texas community colleges.

When the literacy project was completed in 1982, she continued working with John on other research projects and writing about successful initiatives and programs in teaching and learning. Many observers credit Suanne with making a significant contribution to the field of developmental education during this period. She was considered to be "a leading national consultant on remedial programs."[2]

"She was probably the first voice for underprepared students," says Robert McCabe, former president of Miami Dade Community College. "She was the first to look at developmental education and say, 'We have to do better—this is important.' She brought focus to this issue."[3]

She has been characterized as the "carrier of the torch for developmental education and for the student who has been left behind."[4] "John and Suanne Roueche have arguably been the longest and strongest champions of quality developmental education."[5] She coauthored a best-selling textbook, *Awareness: Exercises in Basic Composition Skills* in 1972, and between 1969 and 1990, she gave dozens of workshops, seminars, and keynote presentations around the country on topics such as "Accommodating Individual Differences," "Design and Evaluation of Effective Developmental Programs," "Attacking the Literacy Problem," and "College Responses to Low-Achieving Students."

Meanwhile, the service arm of the CCLP, the National Institute for Staff and Organizational Development (NISOD), had begun to make a mark on the professional and staff development scene on campuses of its community college members across the United States and Canada.

However, over a five-year period NISOD had enjoyed the service of four different directors, each of whom had been "picked off" to head other programs or assume positions elsewhere. As well, the organization was in transition, considering and then implementing some major organizational changes and membership services.

ASSUMES THE LEADERSHIP OF NISOD

It was clear that NISOD needed a director who would remain in the position long enough to oversee these new developments. So, as yet another director was announcing departure, and in a meeting to discuss NISOD's future, the dean of the College of Education suggested to John that Suanne would be just the person—by training, reputation, and experience—to take on the assignment. However, as NISOD's directors had each reported to John, the university's strict nepotism rules would prohibit the appointment, so the dean advised: "Tell her that she'll just report to me!"[6]

As Suanne had been editing NISOD's *Innovation Abstracts* and serving in a support role at its annual conferences on a part-time basis for several months, she jumped at the chance to do such challenging and creative work full-time. As NISOD director, she assisted John and NISOD's existing staff in evaluating its existing programs, paring down some, eliminating a few, and enhancing others.

NISOD's annual conference, the International Conference on Teaching Excellence, was drawing several hundred attendees in its early days. Under Suanne's leadership, the conference expanded and grew; attendance rose to well above the thousand attendance mark fairly quickly and reached the two thousand mark by May 2000. Membership in NISOD had grown from fifty-two colleges to more than six hundred by the time Suanne retired in 2001.

Initially funded by the W. K. Kellogg Foundation and the Fund for the Improvement of Postsecondary Education, NISOD became a self-supporting entity earlier than anticipated. By providing timely teaching tips in practitioner-written articles in a weekly publication, *Innovation Abstracts*, and hosting an excellent professional development experience every May in Austin (the NISOD annual conference expanded its name to become the International Conference on Teaching and Leadership Excellence), NISOD developed a reputation for making a difference in community college teaching and learning—helping disseminate, promote, and support best practices into college classrooms across North America.

George Boggs, former college president before becoming president of the American Association of Community Colleges (AACC), characterizes the NISOD conference as a place where "bright, energetic faculty come together in one place and get recognized."[7] "It is aimed at improving learning and teaching in the classroom. It's an outstanding experience," says a former AACC president, David Pierce.[8] Robert Sandel recalls that when he started his presidency at Mountain Empire Community College (Virginia),

> I was looking for a program that made a difference for *teaching*, and I decided upon NISOD after talking to colleagues. Each year we chose a group of faculty to honor, gave them a monetary award, and took them to Austin as a team. There they met Suanne Roueche, listened to her philosophy and the impact that community colleges were having on various constituencies around the country. NISOD was a proactive program that really impacted the faculty. I saw how enthused and excited our faculty were by NISOD and how it made a difference in the classroom.[9]

K. Patricia Cross believes that the NISOD conference is important because it recognizes the teaching function of community colleges by centering it on presenters who have been identified as excellent teachers. NISOD's popularity grew not only because of the substance of the sessions, but, with Suanne's touch, began to incorporate social events—including a Mexican buffet and country-western dance—so that "people would have a good time" in and around having an excellent—and memorable—professional development experience.

In 1990, the NISOD conference began to recognize individuals selected by their colleges as outstanding staff, faculty, and administrators who had made a difference in the life of the college. Recipients of the NISOD Excellence Award are presented with a medallion, suitable for wearing to college official functions and displaying in their offices.

SPEAKER, TEACHER, AND AUTHOR

Suanne is widely praised for her speaking ability. "Once you hear her speak and see the real excitement that she has, it is contagious."[10] Between 1969 and 2001, she spoke before 122 audiences, including community colleges, universities, and national organizations.

Deserved or not, many give her credit for much of the success of the Community College Leadership Program, particularly its success in graduating large numbers of women and minorities. "John's center has lived out the eras, whereas others have weakened or were never as strong.

Suanne was kind of in the background of the program, behind the scenes," believes former Maricopa chancellor Paul Elsner.[11] Others characterize their relationship as John's being the driving force and Suanne's being the supportive partner.

John praises Suanne's excellence as a teacher, particularly her role in creating the exemplary developmental program at El Centro in the 1970s. And, he adds, it was her inspiration for NISOD to "get useful, practical advice into hands of teachers."[12] *Innovation Abstracts* rapidly became one of the most influential with the largest circulation of publications in higher education—more than eighty-five thousand copies were mailed weekly to NISOD member colleges.

Many have neither attended NISOD nor were around during the time Suanne was active in developmental education. Nonetheless, her name is a community college household word because of her prolific coauthorship of books in the field. Her publications are practically guaranteed best sellers for the Community College Press, reported AACC's George Boggs.[13]

In describing the process of writing together, John Roueche says, "Suanne is the wordsmith; I am more forceful. We are all together on what needs to be said. She is the best writer I have ever been around."[14] Virtually never the solo author on a book, chapter, or article, Suanne describes a process with her coauthors whereby they jointly agree about the topic and points, with John often supplying the kernel of all ideas.

She then becomes the one "sitting in front of the computer," mapping out the chapters and wielding the fresh brush of writing. After consultation over the drafts, she makes changes, talking with John or other coauthors along the way. She is most proud of the fact that her writing focuses on successful practices. She prides herself in "writing about things that are useful." "I choose my words carefully and work hard to engage the reader."

Suanne's service to community college education spanned almost four decades. She continued in semiretirement as senior lecturer in the Department of Educational Administration at UT and publications editor for NISOD. Despite working only eight years in a community college, her experience served as solid grounding for the numerous publications, speeches, and conferences that have helped others improve their teaching.

In the end, Suanne believes she made a unique contribution to the movement, through "writing about successful practices, and celebrating and showcasing people, programs, and teaching strategies that work."

Chapter Eleven

Wilhelmina Delco

Voice for Education's Underrepresented

Wilhelmina Delco

Although nationally active between 1975 and 1994 in "every organization that had 'education' in its name,"[1] Wilhelmina Delco's prominence on the community college scene was relatively brief. But the role she played in helping community colleges understand the political perspective—and particularly in raising consciousness about their responsibility to black students—had significant impact. Wilhelmina's keen analytic skills and savvy political sense allowed her to shape higher education policy at the city, state, and national levels.

——— ⌘ ———

Born in 1929, Wilhelmina Ruth Fitzgerald Delco's background and accomplishments have been the subject of numerous articles and chapters in books,[2] and they are colorful in the telling. In short, hers is the story of a girl raised by a dynamic, divorced working mother, Juanita Health Fitzgerald, in a housing project in Chicago as one of five children.

Her mother imparted philosophies of life to her children, influencing her bright young daughter Wilhelmina to set her sights high. "My mother always said to us, 'We are not poor—we just have no money. The reason you go to school is so that you will have some money.' That always struck me, because then poverty becomes an attitude rather than a financial statement." Wilhelmina chose sociology as her major when she decided to go to college, influenced by what she had observed while tagging along to work with her mother, who was a probation officer.

At Fisk University, she met her future husband, Exalton A. Delco, Jr., and moved with him to Austin, where he was pursuing a doctorate at University of Texas. Despite his status as a graduate student, the Delcos were denied married-student housing because they were black. Instead, they were offered residence in a housing project, which they refused. They then learned of housing at Huston-Tillitson College (a historically black college); Exalton eventually spent much of his teaching and administrative career at Huston-Tillitson.[3]

BECOMES POLITICALLY ACTIVE

Despite the fact that she had a bachelor's degree, Wilhelmina, unlike most black women of that era, chose not to work outside the home. She had heard during a marriage-preparation class that "the biggest contributing factor of teenage pregnancy was having no one at home to talk to, and therefore we decided I would always be there" for their children.

The Delcos settled in East Austin and had three daughters and one son. She became active in her children's school and extracurricular activities. Her frustration with being told that her Girl Scout troop would have to pay for janitorial services for use of a school led her in 1968 to run for the Austin Independent School Board. In addition, she was bothered by the homogeneity of the school board.

At the time, of the seven school board members, four of them lived within five blocks of each other. They could have met at 7-11 and had a quorum! I ran on a platform of broader representation, broader education, and broader communication. That was my euphemism for saying that it ought to go beyond that little community; it ought to reach out.[4]

She was elected on her first try as the first African American member of the school board.[5] She attributes her victory to the fact that she had the support of the League of Women Voters and that the election was held just days after the assassination of the Reverend Dr. Martin Luther King Jr. Her election was noteworthy because she represented the black side of a geographically segregated Austin. "Those of us who live in East Austin called Interstate 35 the 'Red Sea.' Crossing the interstate took an act of God."

In 1972, during her tenure on the school board, the state asked that the board seek authority from the voters to establish a community college in Austin. Although she had no personal experience with junior or community colleges, Wilhelmina was struck by the fact "that over half of the students entering higher education nationally were at community colleges—so for many of our people, that was the access route because private higher education was very expensive. . . . Community colleges represented a viable alternative: they were closer, cheaper, and more flexible. They seemed to be an avenue for hope."

Wilhelmina campaigned for the proposal for a community college, touting what she called the "five facets: 1) the first two years toward the baccalaureate, 2) credentialing for vocational-technical skills beyond high school, 3) 'respectable entry' for people who had dropped out (e.g., GED), 4) continuing education and training for business, and 5) personal enrichment." When the voters authorized the college but defeated funding for it, Wilhelmina and her colleagues on the school board became the de facto governing board for the new Austin Community College.

Wilhelmina quickly concluded that the real power for educational decision making rested not in the local school boards but in the state legislature. Of particular interest to her was the ruling in *Rodríguez et al. v. San Antonio ISD*, a class-action suit, in which a federal district court declared the Texas school-finance system unconstitutional.[6] Explaining why she chose to run for the legislature, she said, "I wanted to solve public-school finance issues and get out of there."[7]

In 1974, she won a seat on the Texas House of Representatives, making her the first African American to be elected at-large in Travis County (greater Austin).[8] By her third term, she had been appointed chair of the Higher Education Committee for the House of Representatives and served in that capacity until her selection as speaker pro tempore in 1991. As chair of the Higher Education Committee, "she carried major pieces of legislation that affected community colleges and historically black colleges and universities in the state."[9]

APPOINTED TO THE AACJC FUTURES COMMISSION

By this time, Wilhelmina's accomplishments and leadership capabilities had caught the attention of national groups. Among numerous appointments, she served on the board and as chair of the Educational Testing Service, where she had the chance to interact with Ernest L. Boyer, then president of the Carnegie Foundation for the Advancement of Teaching.

Apparently impressed with Mrs. Delco, Boyer suggested to Dale Parnell that she be named to AACJC's Futures Commission, which Parnell had asked Boyer to chair. Created by Parnell in 1987, the commission was "to develop recommendations about where community colleges should be headed in the next century."[10] Wilhelmina certainly had the credentials to make a substantive contribution—by this time she was chair of the Texas House Higher Education Committee, and her husband was an administrator at Austin Community College.

The board appointed nineteen members to the prestigious Futures Commission,[11] and its work became an important focal point for AACJC for several years. Through her membership on the commission, Wilhelmina quickly developed a reputation for being "an advocate for women and minority rights, in many ways. She was very outspoken about those things. We did not have a black woman advocate who spoke as passionately and concisely as she did."[12]

PUSHES AACJC ON ISSUES OF
ACCESS AND EQUAL OPPORTUNITY

At the time, AACJC was experiencing something of a crisis of legitimacy among the African American leaders in its membership, some of whom felt "neglected or ignored by the association."[13] And "some members of the Futures Commission wanted to gloss over words such as 'access,' and 'equal opportunity,'" recalls Connie Sutton-Odems, AACJC's then-vice president. Some members of the commission believed "that these were not issues, but [Delco] pushed them. The commission was not opposed to [these issues] being part of the report, but they were sensitive to how the field was going to look at that. It's one thing to say, 'It's important,' and another to say, 'Here are the attitudes and policies that need to be changed.'"[14]

To this day, Wilhelmina believes the most important idea from the Futures Commission was one that originated with Ernest Boyer. "'*Community* means more than a region to be served, but a climate to be created.' I love that—it says it all. It's a climate that creates community involvement in the process of improving the community and enhancing the quality of that community through education. And the community college, if it's doing its job, ought to reach into every home in the community."

After the Futures Commission's report, *Building Communities: A Vision for a New Century*, was adopted, the AACJC board decided to follow up on several recommendations in the report on minorities and access. According to Wilhelmina, the AACJC Black Caucus said that they "had watched me on the commission, and I would raise all the key questions that, unless they were willing to jeopardize their jobs, they couldn't ask. But I had no job—I never worked for any of them. So they recommended me to lead this effort."

Thus, Wilhelmina was appointed chair of the Commission on Minority Concerns, to oversee the Minority Education Initiative, which was "designed to assist colleges with the adoption of aggressive policies to improve recruitment and retention of minority students and faculty."[15] As a result of the commission's recommendations, AACJC established an Office of Minority Affairs Concerns. Although not generally acknowledged as a key report in the history of AACJC, the Minorities in Education report allowed, at the very least, the perception among those in the field that this was an important issue to AACJC.

By virtue of her work on these and other commissions, and her many speaking engagements, she was perceived to be in a central leadership role at AACJC during those years. More than her emphasis on minority issues, community college leaders were impressed with the fact that a state legislative leader would choose to contribute to AACJC's work.

"She was strong, and her ideas were from outside education—that helped us understand our perspectives better. She helped bring up issues of underserved populations," recalls Beverly Simone, who served with her on the Futures Commission.[16]

Peppering her speeches with aphorisms and humorous self-deprecation, Mrs. Delco's oratorical skills were legendary. Not only did she "get you excited listening to her talk,"[17] but she also was a "compelling speaker"[18] and always "a champion for underprepared students."[19]

HELPS LEGITIMATE COMMUNITY COLLEGES IN THE AFRICAN AMERICAN COMMUNITY

For the black leadership in community colleges, she was "a number-one role model politically and educationally."[20] "She was able to take on areas of controversy, set forward goals, and get people working. Her approach was very candid, straightforward, with a velvet touch. Getting something done was more important than making a lot of noise."[21] She was

> a rare political leader who chose to be actively involved in community colleges. She contributed on the thought side on a whole range of task forces, commissions, and so forth. Her decision to be actively engaged as a state legislator was a breath of fresh air to those of us choosing to run colleges to understand the legislative perspective. She brought the perspective and realities from the state legislature to those in community colleges in those meetings and dialogues.[22]

"Along with Connie Odems, she helped bring legitimacy to community colleges in the African American community," believes Dale Parnell.[23] More than that, she "made black women look at the possibility of leadership in a different way. She had a bully pulpit and wasn't afraid to say things that needed to be said. She believed in the structural changes that needed to take place in community colleges, through improved access."[24]

Wilhelmina's belief in community colleges was more than superficial. She had a strong message for all community college leaders about the dearth of minorities in community colleges.

You have to sell this concept. *You* have to sell this institution. *You* have to show them where it's worth *their* effort to submit themselves to what *you* say can make a difference in their lives. *You* have to make the case. That's what I kept pushing.

She was a "highly regarded and visible spokeswoman"[25] both for the promise of community colleges and for disadvantaged citizens. She "was everywhere"[26] during those years. "As an active legislator from a large state with active community college programs, people listened to her. She was a charming speaker who could persuade people of her commitments."[27]

Delco was honored with the AACC National Leadership Award in 1991. When asked what contribution she made through her prodigious work and service, she replies, "I can keep them honest. They will never again be able to say about the problems and issues in my community that they 'didn't know.' My job is to tell them." She certainly left that legacy with America's community college movement.

Chapter Twelve

Women of the Tribal Colleges

Extending the Model

During the period when hundreds of new community colleges were opening and experiencing phenomenal growth, a parallel model was being spawned, largely in the West and Midwest, among American Indian populations. Soon after the Navajo Tribal Council founded its own community college in 1968, other Indian tribes followed suit.

Yet this movement, grounded in the principle of self-determination, receives scant reference in mainstream community college literature. The editor of the *Tribal College Journal* articulated this point in 2002: "Yet for some reason these [faculty and administrators] at the 33 tribal colleges and universities in the American Indian Higher Education Consortium seem to be invisible to the rest of the country as they quietly go about their work of changing lives."[1]

Two of the four women described in this chapter helped found or lead early tribal colleges; one had a hand in shaping and securing passage of key federal legislation; another was able to marshal extensive private resources to support the cause.

RUTH ROESSEL: FOUNDING OF
THE FIRST TRIBAL COLLEGE

Ruth Wheeler grew up on the Navajo reservation in northeast Arizona. She met Robert (Bob) A. Roessel Jr. in 1952 when he was teaching on the reservation at a school in Round Rock, Arizona. Despite their cultural differences—he was white—they were married with Ruth's parents' blessing in 1955. Speaking only Navajo until age eleven, Ruth went on to obtain

Ruth Roessel

a bachelor's degree in elementary education at Arizona State University (ASU) after marrying Bob, and later her master's in Indian studies at ASU.

Bob and Ruth settled in Red Rock on the reservation, where they made numerous contributions to the education and culture of the Navajo peoples over the next four decades. One of their early innovations was to help establish and run Rough Rock Demonstration School, among the first efforts to prove to the U.S. Bureau of Indian Affairs (BIA) that the Navajo could run their own school.

Buoyed by the success of this endeavor, and knowing firsthand the difficulties inherent in Navajos having to move to Tempe to attend college at ASU (the nearest public university), as early as 1959 Ruth planted the idea of starting an Indian-run college on the reservation.

Supported by the chairman of the Navajo Nation, Raymond Nakai, and other tribal and local BIA officials, the Roessels convinced the Navajo tribal council that the time was ripe to found a community college—one that would be located on the reservation and geared to the needs of the Navajo people.[2]

The need was manifest: the average number of school years Navajo adults completed was less than three; 70 percent of adults did not read, write, or speak English; and only 10 percent of Navajo college-scholarship recipients completed a degree.[3] Statistics showed that nationally,

90 percent of Native Americans who pursued higher education did not graduate.[4] Homesickness, culture shock, financial woes, and inadequate academic preparation were thought to be among the challenges to successful retention in college.

In the Roessels' vision, the new college would mirror the functions of other community colleges, offering adult, transfer, and vocational-technical education. In addition, the college would seek to "foster the development and preservation of a healthy pride among Navajo people in their heritage; and . . . serve as a center for development of Indian cultures, with a special emphasis on the Navajo."[5]

Authorized by the tribal council in 1968, the college first operated out of the BIA high school in Many Farms, Arizona. College officials soon sought a permanent location for the new college, one more centrally located in the heart of the twenty-five thousand square miles of Navajo reservation. But this ambitious vision required financial support—at a level that only the federal government could provide.

The BIA in Washington, D.C., was unsympathetic, and funding did not look promising even after tribal leaders made numerous trips to visit officials such as U.S. Representative Wayne Aspinall from Colorado, then-chairman of the influential House Interior Committee. After making what they believed was their last bid to garner the congressman's support, Bob Roessel and tribal officials were led from his office.

Ruth, however, lagged behind and seized the moment. "We're going to have a groundbreaking. Would you like to come?" Responding to his apparent interest, Ruth went on to describe how the ceremony would resemble that used when building a Navajo home, involving a medicine man and offering of turquoise stones. Intrigued, Aspinall responded that he'd be there.

At the groundbreaking, Aspinall and several others held the gish, the traditional digging stick. During the lengthy ceremony, Bob Roessel grew increasingly alarmed. The day was hot; the congressman was elderly; and Aspinall was stooped over, his hands below the others on the gish. At the end, he released the stick and slowly stood up, calling Bob Roessel to his side. "I have been to the mosques; I have been to synagogues; I've been to churches all over the world. But I felt God when I felt that stick. You will get your college," he said. True to his word, Aspinall shouted down Congressional and Bureau of Indian Affairs opponents, and the Navajo Community College Act of 1971 became law.[6]

Ruth's career at the college included teaching and administration for the next twelve years. At the same time, she and Bob reared five children and perpetuated Navajo culture and traditions through numerous avenues.

Although her husband remained more visible and active in the life of Navajo Community College,[7] initially it was Ruth who gave him the "connection to the family," in this case, the Salt Clan Family, an extended family system. "You have to establish connections with the people, and the clan system is very important for making connections with the community and to the tribe," explains Johnson Bia, an educator who grew up on the Navajo reservation. The Roessels are credited with being "instrumental in changing the face of education on the Navajo Reservation."[8] Ruth died in 2012.

HELEN MAYNOR SCHEIRBECK:
ORGANIZING FOR FEDERAL SUPPORT

By word of mouth, the developments in the Navajo reservation caught the attention of other Indian leaders. The model of the American community college appealed to them. "Their philosophy of open admission, job training, and community development closely matched the needs of

Helen Maynor Scheirbeck

reservations,"[9] according to Paul Boyer, who documented the movement during its early years.

One of the first people to recognize that the future of the tribal-college movement depended upon federal funding—such as Navajo Community College had obtained—was Helen Maynor Scheirbeck, then-director of the Office of Indian Affairs in the U.S. Department of Health, Education, and Welfare. Born in 1935 in North Carolina, Helen was a member of the Lumbee tribe. From prior experiences, Helen had come to believe that "Indian people had to control the institutions and resources available to them before they could begin the long journey toward self-sufficiency."[10]

To help implement that belief, in 1972 Helen convened a meeting in Washington, D.C., of educators affiliated with nascent tribal colleges. During that and subsequent meetings, Helen urged them to form an alliance to aid in getting access to federal money.[11] Subsequently, presidents from six of the first colleges[12] gathered in Denver in 1973 and founded the American Indian Higher Education Consortium (AIHEC), whose goals included passage and funding of federal legislation to support the burgeoning tribal-college movement.[13]

In the meantime, Helen worked with other Department of Education officials to gain access to Title III (developing institutions) as a start-up source of funding for the colleges.[14] "I knew how to work the bureaucracy," recalls Helen.

> I was in the bureaucracy after passage of the Navajo Community College legislation. We then had to "make it real" inside the bureaucracy. I asked the Commissioner [of Education, Sidney Marland] if I could shepherd it through the bureaucracy. What I did was sit and talk with people in the various areas such as financial aid so that I could learn their attitude toward this concept and then help get their support for it. This helped when we started moving the tribal college legislation through.[15]

To obtain more stable funding, Helen recommended that AIHEC go after its own legislation, modeled on the federal law supporting Navajo Community College. AIHEC requested Helen's assistance in drafting the legislation and followed her advice on how to secure cosponsors and to introduce it in both the House and the Senate.[16]

During the long drive for passage of legislation, Helen also wrote an influential report for AIHEC examining the federal educational authorities for potential legislative authority to fund tribal colleges.[17] For years after its eventual passage,[18] Helen could be counted on for help with legislation, to reach a congressman, or to lend her voice.[19]

Now remembered as "an important advocate in helping launch the tribal-college movement,"[20] Helen went on to play prominent roles in K–12 Indian education, Indian Head Start, and later, the founding of the Smithsonian Institution's National Museum of the American Indian. "We have our own Rosa Parks here," remarked a former colleague. "Helen Scheirbeck has changed history by altering Washington, D.C.'s, attitude toward Indian people."[21]

JANINE PEASE: GROWING THE
TRIBAL COLLEGE MOVEMENT

Although a number of women—both Indian and non-Indian—held leadership positions in tribal colleges in the decades after Congress made federal funding available, one women served as a beacon of inspiration and as a prominent spokesperson for the movement. Janine Pease[22] is a Crow and Hidatsa Indian, born in 1949 and enrolled in the Crow Tribe of Indians.

Janine Pease

Beginning her career as a counselor at Navajo Community College and director of the first adult education program on the Crow Reservation, she went on to become the founding president of Little Big Horn College (LBHC; Montana) in 1982 and served in that capacity for eighteen years. During her presidency, LBHC grew from thirty to three hundred students, received regional accreditation, built a comprehensive curriculum around the Crow Indian language and culture, and built a campus facility. She received a master's and doctorate from Montana State University.

More than the head of a single college, Janine is acknowledged as a national leader in the tribal college movement during its crucial early years. Often described as "charismatic," Janine's height at six feet made her stand out for more than her ideas. "She received a lot of fame and attention" during that era.[23] "She somehow came to personify tribal colleges—by the way she looks and speaks—with passion, and from the heart."[24]

Before Congress, she was able to articulate the vision for tribal colleges and led the American Indian Highter Education Consortium (AIHEC) to success on the Hill. "Of all the women in the tribal college movement, she had the longest-lasting ability to move people in D.C., getting money. She was hooked into the D.C. power network like you've never seen. She is extremely bright, and photogenic. She is seen as the role model for those who came after her."[25]

Equally important, Janine was instrumental in building the effectiveness of AIHEC. She was able to "get people to unify around concepts and helped get AIHEC solidly put together,"[26] as member colleges needed to rely on each other to solve problems and build programs.

Janine's ability to articulate well the case for tribal colleges is seen in this response to a question during a 1991 magazine interview:

> One of the reasons tribal colleges have been effective in their own communities is that the structures they provide have not been offensive or invasive to the tribal communities, but rather are complementary. That is, tribal colleges have tried to utilize the methods of organization from their own communities. . . . And so it's much more an organization of the people than if you were to transport some community college from outside into downtown Crow Agency.[27]

Janine's contributions led to honorary academic degrees and numerous recognitions, including being named in 1990 as National Indian Educator of the Year by the National Indian Education Association, receiving a

MacArthur Foundation Fellowship Award in 1994, and being appointed by President Clinton to several advisory councils.

BARBARA BRATONE: ESTABLISHING THE AMERICAN INDIAN COLLEGE FUND

By the late 1980s, more than twenty-five tribal colleges had been established and were receiving federal funding. But the movement needed greater resources to support scholarships, facilities, and programs. Piggybacking on the success of the United Negro College Fund, in 1989 the tribal college presidents launched the American Indian College Fund (AICF). They hoped to draw support from corporations and foundations for student scholarships and program initiatives.

Within a few years, the fund was receiving generous contributions from individuals and corporations. Key to its rapid success was the choice of Barbara Bratone as its first executive director.

First in her family to go to college, Barbara became a teacher after completing her degree at the State University of New York at Cortland in 1963. One of the "first wave of women to go back to work"[28] after getting

Barbara Bratone

married and raising a family, Barbara found that her previous work as a community volunteer served her well in getting back into the workforce.

After working as a "start-up" person for a number of organizations focused on programs for racial minorities, she landed a fund-raising job with the Phelps Stokes Foundation in New York City and became well connected with its philanthropic community. As the Stokes Foundation always included an American Indian on its board, Barbara became acquainted with various national American Indian leaders in the early 1970s. So she was not surprised when they approached her about serving as the director of a new operation that they hoped would raise much-needed cash for the struggling colleges.

"We hired Barbara as our executive director to put together a group of wealthy, influential people for our board," recalls Jim Shanley of Fort Peck Community College (Montana).[29] Most remarkably, although the precursor United Negro College Fund could have seen this new organization as its competition, Barbara "got the United Negro College Fund to support the founding of the American Indian College Fund."[30]

Accomplishments of the AICF during Barbara's directorship included a highly successful direct-mail campaign, a pro bono marketing campaign from a prestigious ad agency, and receipt of $800,000 a year over three years in donations from Pew Charitable Trust, Lilly Endowment, and the U.S. West, Ford, Rockefeller, and MacArthur Foundations during the AICF's initial years of operation. Through her fund-raising efforts, each tribal college received $1 million to support sorely needed campus construction projects.[31]

Barbara is acknowledged for her insistence that tribal college leaders drive the organization and for grooming promising American Indians to assume key leadership roles. Barbara, who is white, "always tried to make sure American Indian people got to be the spokesmen," reports Jim Shanley.[32] In 1995, she turned over the executive directorship to an American Indian.

Although Barbara attributes the remarkable successes under her leadership to "being in the right place at the right time," others in the movement give her direct credit. "We went on to do some remarkable things [after hiring Barbara]. All our building funds started with what Barbara began. Her understanding of the philanthropic world made all the difference."

"Barbara put her heart and soul into something people said would never work," reflects Martha McLeod, a tribal college president from that era.

In 2002, Barbara was honored with a Lifetime Achievement Award by the fund for her "tireless and successful work as the former executive director."

A REMARKABLE LEGACY

Tribal colleges—which today number thirty-seven (with seventy-five campuses in sixteen states) and enroll some eighteen thousand students in credit-bearing courses[33]—owe a large debt to a number of women, only a few of whom were described in this chapter. "More than most higher-education movements, women—especially Indian women—were very important" to the establishment and growth of tribal colleges, believes Wayne Stein, director of the Center for Native American Studies at Montana State University, Bozeman.[34]

A number of other women played pivotal roles in the movement's early years: Carol Davis, early instigator, along with Twila Martin, of Turtle Mountain Community College (North Dakota); Margaret Campbell Perez, an early president of Fort Belknap Community College (Montana); Verna Fowler, founding president of College of Menominee (Wisconsin); Veronica Gonzales, longtime executive director of AIHEC; Phyllis Howard, cofounder of Fort Berthold Community College (North Dakota); Patricia Locke of the Western Interstate Commission on Higher Education; Martha McLeod, long-serving president of Bay Mills Community College (Michigan); and Peggy Nagel, a founder of Stone Child College (Montana).

"Maybe . . . one of the reasons that our colleges have more women [administrators than in the rest of higher education] is because we can advance professionally while living within our family support systems," speculates Cheryl Crazy Bull.[35]

Moreover, from the beginning of the tribal college movement, the majority of students were women. The typical tribal college student was often described as a single mother in her early thirties. Tribal college officials explain that this population was the least served by higher education, yet was the most eager to get a degree. "Women with children, especially, are often determined to get off welfare and provide for their families, but are unable or unwilling to leave home and attend schools in distance cities. For them, tribal colleges were the only option."[36]

Jim Shanley, a major player himself in the tribal college movement, pays tribute to the American Indian women who make up the majority of the staff at the colleges. "They do the day-to-day things that we need to get done on the reservation."[37] Asked why women are so well represented on the staff and faculty of tribal colleges, one administrator stated, "A woman who manages a household is accustomed to operating on a minimal budget. It takes a lot of sacrifice. That's what I see as really abundant in Native American women. They seek to make improvements. Their hearts, their minds, and their souls are positive."[38]

Indeed, Ruth Roessel, Helen Scheirbeck, Janine Pease, and Barbara Bratone are but four of the women who, through their contributions to the tribal college movement, helped American Indian peoples take this positive, significant step toward educational self-determination.

Part III

REFLECTIONS

In her book, *Composing a Life*, Mary Catherine Bateson writes:

> The women's history movement has many different elements . . . : the need
> to make the invisible visible, the desire to provide role models and empower
> aspirations, the possibility that by setting a number of life histories side by
> side, we will be enabled to recognize common patterns of creativity that
> have not been acknowledged or fostered.[1]

This section attempts to do just that: to view the lives of these sixteen
influential women together, so as to discern patterns that helped or
hindered them in their journey toward making singular contributions
to the community college movement.[2] Through this analysis of their
life stories, readers might more fully understand what it takes to make
an impact through one's professional contributions. Important insights,
gleaned from the experiences of these women, might well guide and
inspire those who follow.

WHAT DID NOT SEEM TO MATTER

Were these women, for instance, advantaged by their family backgrounds? It does not appear that having educated or "involved" parents
was a necessary condition for their success.

By and large, these women came from modest family backgrounds.
Two were daughters of university professors, and the father of one was a
successful clothing manufacturer; the professions of other fathers included

minister, nurseryman, farmer, and laborer. None had mothers with careers outside the home after starting a family, with the exception of Wilhelmina Delco, whose mother supported her family by working as a probation officer. Most of the mothers were not college educated.

Suanne Roueche, Connie Sutton-Odems, and Wilhelmina Delco are the only three who attributed gaining their sense of self from a family member. Suanne's grandmother "simply led me to believe that I was capable of doing and being anything I wanted." Recalls Connie, "As near as I can remember, growing up I was taught that I could be whatever I wanted to be." "I inherited my stick-to-itiveness and the sense of self from my mother," says Wilhelmina. "She used to say, 'For some people, the slums are in them. And for others, they're just temporarily in the slums.'"

Being from modest family backgrounds, almost all talked about their sacrifices due to lack of finances at some point, usually in their twenties:

- Margaret Mosal, having been left a widow at forty-three, traveled more than two hours to work in a suitable job to provide for her family.
- Marie Martin's graduation from Berkeley, at the beginning of the Great Depression, compelled her to work as a stenographer.
- When completion of her master's program coincided with a tight job market due to the Korean War, Mildred Montag worked in secretarial positions to support herself. She had to sell her car in order to return to graduate school. "I studied for my doctorate part-time because making a living was a necessity," she recalled.
- Pat Cross altered her dream of attending the University of Illinois in deference to her family's argument that by attending a perfectly good local university, she could save money by living at home. She decided not to transfer in her junior year because she would have had to pay back a scholarship that supported her in her first two years.
- Dorothy Knoell's completion of her dissertation was delayed for a year while she earned money to have it typed.
- Mildred Bulpitt chose one graduate school over another because it offered her a more lucrative assistantship.
- Recently divorced and rearing two sons, Janet Lieberman's expenses for the last year of her doctoral program were paid for by a friend of her mother.

Most of the sixteen women fended for themselves financially for short or long periods of time—this in an era when most women relied upon the income of a spouse. Did it have a dampening effect on their lives? Despite the hardships, many spoke of these tight times with amusement if not some pride; in retrospect, they realize that these sacrifices along the way were relatively small and did not seriously hinder their ability to succeed in the long run.

Did the career paths of these women require that they be geographically mobile? Not particularly, it appears.

Some of these women, notably Margaret Mosal, Janet Lieberman, Suanne Roueche, and Ruth Roessel, never left their home state. Others, such as Mildred Bulpitt, Carolyn Desjardins, and Mildred Montag, relocated once or twice but then stayed put as they settled into their careers. Some women always knew where "home" was but moved temporarily for a promising opportunity, such as Marie Martin and Jane Matson to Washington, D.C.

A few did enhance their career opportunities by their willingness to move. Connie Sutton-Odems moved from Florida to Iowa to Washington, D.C., in pursuit of ever more-challenging career opportunities. Pat Cross moved between coasts—first New York and New Jersey, then California, then Massachusetts, then California again. And none moved more than Dorothy Knoell (from Chicago to Wisconsin to Texas to Pennsylvania to California to New York, to Washington, D.C., and then permanently to California).

Interestingly, most of these women spent the major portion of their professional careers on the East Coast, West Coast, or in the Southwest. Of the sixteen women, only two worked elsewhere: Margaret Mosal in Mississippi and Janine Pease in Montana. Four were Californians; three each called New York and Arizona home; and two each were based in Texas and Washington, D.C. Granted, these are among the most populous states, but beyond that, the fact that so many women called California and New York home might be explained by the preeminent role those states played in the evolution of higher education from the 1960s through the 1980s.

Did these women find it challenging to balance their personal and professional lives? Few of the subjects mentioned personal circumstances that adversely affected their professional success.

For the nearly half who did not marry, presumably the pressure to balance demands of their personal and professional lives was less. Possibly the lack of daily family demands gave certain freedom to those who never married—Jane Matson, Pat Cross, and Dorothy Knoell—to travel extensively and to relocate for new positions or temporary assignments. Suanne Roueche "never thought about" the balance, as her daughter and stepson "were easy kids to raise, and we kept them busy. John raised the children with me; he stayed actively involved in their lives."

On the other hand, rearing children had significant implications for a few of the women. Margaret Mosal, a widow, chose to run Phi Theta Kappa Honorary Society out of her hometown in Mississippi in order to stay with her children. Janet Lieberman did not work full-time until after her children were in school. Carolyn Desjardins and Marie Martin did not become active nationally until after they were no longer married and their children were grown.

Mildred Bulpitt and Jane Matson became primary caregivers for their aging mothers, and Wilhelmina Delco cared for both her mother and mother-in-law in her home until their deaths. None mentioned these caregiving roles as detracting from their work.

The women of the tribal colleges often married, reared families, and completed their doctorates while playing leadership roles in their communities. Tribal college administrators often work on their home reservations, with their children living at home. It is not uncommon for extended family members to help take care of the children. One administrator reflected, "Maybe that is one of the reasons that our colleges have more women. We can advance professionally while also living within our family support systems."[3]

The period this book covers encompasses a time of tremendous change in racial and gender equality. Because women were in the minority of those achieving national visibility during this time, might their life stories provide ample evidence of sexual discrimination, or (for the three subjects who are black or Jewish) racial or ethnic prejudice?[4]

Indeed, gender stereotypes significantly influenced the choice of college majors for several women. Carolyn Desjardins wanted to major in history at Weber State College, but she was told that she couldn't because anyone who teaches history had to be able to coach a sport. Connie Sutton-Odems, on the other hand, consciously chose mathematics as a major because "they kept saying, 'Girls don't major in math—you're not supposed to be good in math . . .' so it was kind of my show-me thing." A professor told her that engineering—her long-range goal—was not a field for women.

Janet Lieberman, the only Jewish woman among those profiled, experienced anti-Semitism in several forms. Both the Berkeley Institute, where she attended school, and Vassar, where she started college, had "Jewish quotas"—only a certain number of Jews were admitted to each class.

She recalls that, at the time, "anti-Semitism was present but controlled—it was part of the environment in which we grew up." Before vacations, for instance, her father would call around to make sure that they made hotel reservations where Jews were welcome. This kind of treatment, Janet recalls, was taken for granted.

The racial discrimination young Connie Sutton-Odems experienced as a child in Florida was not so subtle. Despite living in a mixed-race neighborhood, much was segregated, including schools and public facilities. She recalls that her parents taught their offspring to turn the other cheek, "to see the good in people." But even as late as the mid-sixties, vestiges of racism remained. She recalled an experience from her days at Miami Dade when she served on a state task force of counselors.

> We went to a resort in Crystal River, Florida. When it came time for dinner, they would not serve us in the restaurant. There was a Jewish guy in our group, and he thought it was because he was there. Anyway, this was the first time this happened to me as an adult. When you are young, your parents protect you from this. It never occurred to me or the white folks I was with that it was because of me . . . we went back and had the most dramatic meeting about what was needed in our colleges.[5]

Mildred Bulpitt has no doubt that her aspirations for higher-level administrative positions often were thwarted by gender discrimination. In 1961, despite the fact that she had been performing the duties of acting head of the Evening College at Phoenix College for a year, she was told that she could not have job because

> [t]hey were looking for a man who had a lot of experience in adult education programming and was active in national organizations. In those days they didn't hesitate to say that. The second semester they interviewed some men but none took it when they found out the details! Finally, I applied and I

think the reason I got the job was that [the supervisor] probably said something like, 'She's been doing it a year already!' So I got it by default, really.
They were looking for a man—they made no bones about it. In fact, one of
the main reasons he gave me was that as head of the evening program you
had to work at night a lot, and I was in danger of getting raped. There was
a lot of garbage that went on in those days.

The first time I applied [for a presidency] was when Maricopa Technical
College was created. Most of the programs they started were ones we had
started in Evening College. I was told they needed someone who could talk
the vocational talk with people. When I applied to head Phoenix College,
around 1973, I was told that I didn't have the "proper father image." You
see, faculty members liked to bring their personal problems to the president,
and I didn't have the proper father image.[6]

On the other hand, a few women acknowledge that the growing awareness
of racial and gender discrimination worked to their advantage along the
way. "I think I benefited from affirmative action because the University
of Chicago was terrific in terms of women and minorities at the doctoral
level," recalls Dorothy Knoell. "I almost never had a problem with men
taking credit for what I did."

Connie Sutton-Odems knows that she caught the attention of Peter Masiko because "they were looking to hire minorities" at Miami Dade. She
also believes that she was hired at AACJC "because it was under pressure
to have more minorities." Wilhelmina Delco attributed her election as the
first black woman to the Austin Independent School Board in 1968 to
the fact that the election was held two days after the assassination of the
Reverend Dr. Martin Luther King Jr.

Perhaps their lack of sensitivity to discriminatory behaviors derives
from their attitudes. Says Connie Sutton-Odems, "I don't go around wearing my race on my shoulder. I don't meet people expecting them to be
racist. So sometimes I probably don't see it." Likewise, Suanne Roueche
stated in response to a question about whether she encountered discrimination, "If I did, I just ignored it. I don't think I believed it."

In retrospect, Janet Lieberman believes these kinds of experiences were
"formative in character and motivation." As her religious training asserted
that Jews were the chosen people, she took this type of discrimination in
stride. Mildred Bulpitt senses that it was perhaps her experiences in being
denied higher-level administrative positions because of her sex that led

her to pursue programs to advance women in leadership. "I did know that something wasn't right," she recalls.

PERSONAL CHARACTERISTICS
THAT SEEMED TO MATTER

Did these women possess specific traits that appear to have helped lead them to positions of prominence? Four stand out clearly.

Desire for Advanced Education

Of the sixteen women, most were the first in their families to attend college. Nonetheless, one (Margaret Mosal) went no further than an associate's degree; two earned only a bachelor's; two, master's degrees; and eleven, doctorates. As only 8 percent of women nationally were completing college in 1960,[7] these well-educated subjects were distinctly in the minority.

Even more impressive is how the eleven women obtained their doctorates. None went sequentially through her bachelor's, master's, and doctorate; all worked at least one year between one degree and another. Many completed their doctorates while working, most full-time. Most seem to have pursued their doctorates, not because they wanted "the credential," but because they loved learning and challenging themselves.

The high level of education these women attained attests to their drive to excel. Few were motivated by the promise of a research professorship after completing their doctorate; in fact, only Jane Matson and Mildred Montag pursued careers in academe. Even those armed with excellent training in research, such as Dorothy Knoell and Pat Cross, knew they would not feel fulfilled simply conducting quantitative research—rather, they were drawn to applying their research to improve educational practice.

Willingness to Seize New Career Opportunities

Young women reading the stories of the rise of these women to prominence might look for patterns in their career paths. Did they pick a field and move progressively upward through the ranks? Did they succeed because they were always willing to take the next step up?

In fact, if their careers have any commonality, it is in the *lack* of linearity in the paths they took. Mildred Bulpitt's early career included several clerical jobs. Pat Cross went from student-personnel administrator, to Educational Testing Service researcher, to university professor. Dorothy Knoell had ten or twelve different positions or assignments, often on soft money. Carolyn Desjardins progressed from counselor to program administrator. Marie Martin worked her way up the ladder in college administration, then vaulted to federal appointee.

Mildred Montag spent most of her career as a faculty member, but she attributed her success to the time she had spent heading a nursing program and working as a nurse educator. Connie Sutton-Odems started as a teacher and moved through positions as a counselor, then program staff, then national association leader. Suanne Roueche was a high school teacher and college faculty member before focusing on research projects and, finally, heading the National Institute for Staff Organizational Development (NISOD). And most of these women interjected their pursuit of the next level of graduate education between these career changes.

Striking in the record of these career changes is the versatility and adaptability of the talents and skills these women displayed. Further, in these career shifts, the always-present possibility of failure in the new endeavor seemed not to deter them from trying something new.

Can these women be considered risk takers? Only one, Dorothy Knoell, addressed this directly. "I've taken risks but have never been without a job." In truth, their behavior might best be described more as "adventurous."

Motivated to Make a Difference

What motivated these women in their careers? It would be surprising to find that these diverse women were driven by similar goals. But in fact, one common thread spins through their stories: a belief in the potential for human or organizational growth and development, and their dedication to making that happen.

For some women, this shared value manifests itself in their dedication to developing the potential of *students*:

• Pat Cross—understanding how to reach the "new student" and adult learner;

- Dorothy Knoell and Janet Lieberman—opening access to at-risk and underserved youth;
- Margaret Mosal—developing programs to increase the sense of self-worth and confidence for high-achieving students;
- Women of the tribal colleges—making possible the promise of relevant higher education to American Indians; and
- Mildred Montag—designing and promoting a better way to prepare nurses.

Others were motivated by developing the potential for adults:

- Mildred Bulpitt and Carolyn Desjardins—women administrators;
- Jane Matson—student-personnel professionals;
- Suanne Roueche—teaching faculty; and
- Connie Sutton-Odems—first, college staff; later, national leaders.

And a few were driven by the bigger picture, emphasizing organizational development:

- Marie Martin—developing capacities of small and rural colleges; and
- Wilhelmina Delco—helping community colleges to see the necessity of embracing all constituents in their communities.

Moreover, these women thrived on their own learning experiences. Connie Sutton-Odems captured this well when she remarked about her new assignment with AACJC, "All of this was stretching me. I was growing and loving it."

To a woman, they insisted on the visible application of their beliefs: they were pragmatic and action oriented. Once they discerned their passion, they possessed tremendous focus on applying it to practice. For instance, once Mildred Bulpitt recognized the lack of women in the pipeline for the presidency, she helped design a solution, and, along with Carolyn Desjardins, started preparing female leaders. Jane Matson was aggressive in insinuating her protégées into student-development leadership positions around the country. Margaret Mosal increased student membership in Phi Theta Kappa and participation in its programs.

Those who conducted research—Pat Cross, Dorothy Knoell, Suanne Roueche, and even Mildred Montag—were insistent that their findings should improve practice. They did not stop with publishing their findings;

they took them on the speaking circuit, worked to influence policy makers, or found grant money to implement them in the field.

Wilhelmina Delco was determined to change policies as they affected black students and staff, through legislation and policy. As she said, "They will never again be able to say about the problems and issues in my community that they 'didn't know.' My job is to tell them." Connie Sutton-Odems worked from within at AACC to increase the number of women and minorities who had a say in decision making. Those who worked within institutions, such as Janet Lieberman and the women of the tribal colleges, designed and implemented programs to improve the outcomes of substantially underserved groups.

These women did not seem motivated by ego gratification. Certainly achieving name recognition and being in demand were not unwelcome, but they did not seem to be motivating factors. Rather, their renown offered opportunities to disseminate their ideas.

Contributing over a Lifespan

In *Writing a Woman's Life*, Carolyn Heilburn suggests, "women are well beyond youth when they begin, often unconsciously, to create another story. Not even then do they recognize it as another story. Usually they believe that the obvious reasons for what they are doing are the only ones; only in hindsight, or through a biographer's imaginative eyes, can the concealed story be surmised."[8]

Certainly this holds true for the subjects of this book: on average, they were in their late forties before achieving visibility on the national scene. Most spent their twenties and thirties exploring career options, working on graduate degrees, or starting families. No one achieved recognition before turning forty, with the exception of Suanne Roueche with her work on developmental education and Janine Pease in her role as college president. Many, including Carolyn Desjardins, Janet Lieberman, Marie Martin, and Jane Matson, were into their fifties before achieving prominence.

For many, it appears that gaining meaningful experiences, buiding self-confidence, and being recognized for their contributions propelled them to the next level of accomplishment or professional upward mobility. None "rested on her laurels" while professionally active.

After retirement, almost all remained active professionally. Because of the recognition they achieved through their work, they continued to be sought after for their insights and professional skills. Marie Martin served as a consultant for presidential searches. Jane Matson consulted for Maricopa Community College on its student-development function and was highly involved as an adviser for Nova Southeastern University. Mildred Montag was a member of the New York State Regents Committee and helped develop an external (distance) associate degree in nursing. She continued to consult with associate degrees in nursing (ADN) programs around the country and give workshops and speeches.

Suanne Roueche retained roles as senior lecturer and editor for NISOD publications. Dorothy Knoell continued writing and consulting for several years after retiring from the California Postsecondary Education Commission, and Janet Lieberman continued to interest foundations in her ideas for expanding access to higher education. Pat Cross remained a sought-after speaker and author, and continued to write and publish books on teaching and learning.

In short, the drive, interests, and intellect that motivated these women throughout their careers did not cease upon retirement. Clearly for them, their work was not a job but a lifelong commitment that continued to energize them.

OTHER FACTORS THAT BENEFITED THEM

Being Mentored

Despite the fact that the notion of mentoring had yet to gain currency during the early years of these women's careers, in telling their stories, many give credit to people who helped them in important ways. Connie Sutton-Odems attributes her move to community colleges and advancement in the ranks to Peter Masiko, the president of then-Miami Dade Junior College. "Pete Masiko was so good to me. I called him my 'great white father.' I was definitely his 'daughter.' He promoted me every chance he got."

Several sources characterize Jane Matson as being mentored by Joseph Fordyce, Terry O'Banion, and James Wattenbarger, who they say had a great deal of influence on Jane's career. Pat Cross considered one of her former professors, Lee J. Cronbach, as a mentor, seeking his advice when she decided to leave student-personnel administration.

Mildred Montag readily identified several women she believed shaped her career, particularly through their insistence that she continue with graduate studies.

> Long before "mentor" and "mentoring" were in common use, Miss Densford [director of the University of Minnesota School of Nursing] was just that for me. It was she who invited me to teach at the university—it was she who prodded me almost daily with the question, "When are you going on?" I have often said that my decision to pursue a master's degree was in self-defense—there was no getting around her questions.[9]

Isabel Stewart, her master's adviser at Teachers College, became another mentor for Mildred. "With Miss Stewart's help I had my degree in one year. It was Miss Stewart who suggested that I consider going on for a doctorate, an idea that hadn't occurred to me. She [suggested a course that] I might be interested in, and I took the course, which was my first step toward the doctorate." Her doctoral adviser, R. Louise McManus, gave Mildred the seeds of the ideas for the associate degree in nursing, and later helped find a publisher for her dissertation and grant money for the pilot program.

Suanne Roueche acknowledges the mentorship of Ruby Herd, who was her department chairperson at El Centro College. "She was very kind to me, and from time to time sent interesting articles my way. Eventually I realized she was saying, 'Here's something that you might try on and see what you can do with this.' She was always promoting things I could think about." Janet Lieberman attributes her understanding of how faculty, working as a team, can come together to deal with student problems, to Pauline Cagen, her principal at the "600" school.

Whether or not they were specifically named as mentors, any number of men played crucial roles in the careers of these women. Charles Hogarth, president of Mississippi College for Women, hired Margaret Mosal in 1954 as the first transfer-admissions counselor for the college despite her lack of prior work experience or a bachelor's degree.

Lee Medsker recognized the talents of Jane Matson, hired her as a counselor at his community college, and fired up her enthusiasm as a community college advocate. Later, Medsker became impressed enough with Dorothy Knoell's work on California's Master Plan for Higher Education that he recruited her to work with him on a national study of transfer students. He also served as a mentor to Pat Cross after he arranged for her to work jointly for ETS and the Center for Research and Development in Higher Education at UC Berkeley.

Edmund Gleazer sought out Connie Sutton-Odems for a vice presidency at AAJCJ; he also found grant money to support research projects for Jane Matson and Dorothy Knoell, among others. State legislator Wilhelmina Delco clearly caught the eye of Ernst Boyer while they were serving on the board of the Educational Testing Service; subsequently, he convinced Dale Parnell to name her to the prestigious Commission on the Future panel.

John Roueche recognized Suanne's potential and encouraged her to get her doctorate, later collaborating with her on developmental education publications. California Community Colleges' Sid Brossman recruited Dorothy Knoell to work for him in the chancellor's office.

The Leaders for the '80s grant would not have been possible without the roles two influential men played. Terry O'Banion was an early champion for increasing the number of women in leadership positions, and, through the League for Innovation, pulled together the women to write the grant to the Fund for the Improvement of Postsecondary Education. Subsequently, the league served as the fiscal agent for the grant, contributing support and publicity. Paul Elsner, chancellor of the Maricopa Community College District, housed the project and subsidized the salaries of the project directors. Their support was critical to this important initiative.

In short, many of these women benefited from the guiding hand of others in positions of importance. In most cases, those others were men— who held the vast majority of leadership positions at the time—who believed and invested in them.

Importance of Timing

One might also conclude that a number of these women benefited from being in the right place at the right time. Connie Sutton-Odems, for instance, states that race played a role in the fact that she was sought out for the AACJC position, as the Black Caucus had aired its grievances on the convention floor the previous year.

Likewise, it is clear that the "rapid rise of the ADN idea depended on the convergence of several urgent needs that came to the forefront of the public consciousness at this time. The immediate occasion for the development of the ADN program was concern over a looming shortage of nurses. . . . A reform movement in nursing intent on moving nursing education into the general system of American higher education was also to play an important role. By the end of the 1940s, conditions were ripe for the emergence of a wholly new, unprecedented way to educate registered nurses."[10] It was at this time that Mildred Montag completed her dissertation, proposing just such a wholly new approach.

Terry O'Banion, one of the architects of the grant that led to the Leaders for the '80s, attributes its success to "the timeliness of the program and the changing needs of society—this program came together at a critical crossroads," he states. Similarly, Suanne Roueche believes that NISOD was "idea whose time had come."

The timing of Dorothy Knoell's seminal research on community college transfer in 1964 "was perfect," believes Pat Cross. "People were beginning to question the standards of community colleges. That [Knoell and Medsker] proved otherwise was really a breakthrough."

And Pat Cross puts significant stock in the timing of her own publications.

> Everything in education goes like this: there's a rise and then there's a dip. I have always planned a book, and by the time an issue hits the absolute top and starts going down, my book is out. It was true with community colleges—the "new student"—this was a rising phenomenon that people weren't paying much attention to yet. It happened with *Adults as Learners* in a dramatic way. That was the time when Walter Mondale had lifelong learning as part of his presidential platform. I didn't invent it or anything—I was just abreast with it. I seem to have picked up the vibrations. The same happened with classroom assessment techniques.[11]

Barbara Bratone thinks that part of the rapid success of the American Indian College Fund was due to its timing. "In the late 1980s, it was 'that time' again." And its inception coincided with the release of the popular film *Dancing with Wolves*, which featured American Indians as actors and the Lakota language. "It helped people see, through popular culture," what needed to be done, she believes.

Despite what appears to be the importance of good timing, these successes were not mere coincidence. These women were actively pursuing what they believed to be important ends, fueled by their own aspirations, their curiosity, their values, and their experiences.

Availability of External Funding Support

In reading these accounts, one is struck by the extent to which federal programs and foundation support helped influence the careers of a number of these women.

- Mildred Montag's dissertation might have languished on a shelf and not resulted in transforming nursing education if it were not for the support of the Russell Sage and W. K. Kellogg Foundations and Mrs. Rockefeller's personal donation.
- The ACCTion Consortium was fully funded, through Marie Martin's help, by federal Title III monies.
- AACJC could not have brought Jane Matson to Washington, D.C., to study student-personnel services in community colleges without the support of the Exxon Educational Foundation.
- The Leaders for the '80s program was made possible by funding from FIPSE, without which potentially fewer women would have been prepared for leadership positions.
- The National Institute for Staff and Organizational Development was created with initial grants from the W. K. Kellogg Foundation and FIPSE.
- Alden Dunham's belief in what Janet Lieberman was proposing at LaGuardia led to his recommending that the Carnegie Corporation support it; the Ford Foundation paid for the eventual dissemination of the middle college model.
- Tribal colleges simply could not have taken off as they did if not for the passage of the federal Tribally Controlled Community College Assistance Act of 1978.
- Funding from the Pew Charitable Trust, Lilly Endowment, and the U.S. West, Ford, Rockefeller, and MacArthur Foundations were key in supporting construction projects at tribal colleges through the American Indian College Fund.

Dorothy Knoell's early career, in particular, was boosted by availability of external funding sources. Lee Medsker brought her in to work on a nationwide study of transfer, supported by a federal grant. Once the study was published, AACJC received a grant to hold conferences to disseminate the findings.

The Ford Foundation supported her research on college enrollment rates for residents of America's cities. And the federal Office of Economic Opportunity funded her to disseminate her findings about educating urban youth and adults at community colleges. Her comment that "untold" federal funds were available to disseminate demonstration projects speaks to the largesse of the federal government during this era.

The "*Sputnik* influence" also figures prominently in several women's careers. In 1957, the launching by the Soviet Union of *Sputnik*—the first earth-orbiting satellite—greatly accelerated a floundering movement to beef up science and mathematics education in the United States. It was believed that the Soviet's demonstrated preeminence in this scientific endeavor threatened the safety and security of America. The federal government lavished money on programs intended to prepare the brightest students for careers in mathematics and the sciences to ensure preparedness against its Cold War nemesis.

Connie Sutton-Odems's career, for one, was aided by this thrust. "The federal government was looking for counselors to direct people into math and science careers. My boss encouraged me to get my master's."[12] She received a scholarship through the National Defense Education Act to attend a graduate program in educational counseling, which presumably emphasized how to encourage students to pursue science and math careers.

Even more importantly, Jane Matson's ability to attract and educate a generation of student services leaders was made possible by the National Defense Education Act. This federal program awarded grants to twelve universities around the country to develop programs to train and educate guidance counselors, in part to encourage students to pursue careers in science and mathematics. It was this grant that allowed Jane to bring the top leaders in the community college movement to speak to her graduate students.

The Attraction of Community Colleges

How did these women find themselves drawn to this relatively new offshoot of higher education? After all, these colleges had yet to gain universal respectability as institutions of higher education. As one of these women, who was considering leaving a faculty position to work at a community college puts it, "Everyone thought I was crazy to take the job. You didn't go from a four-year college to a two-year college."

In general, it seems that these women grasped the potential for what community colleges could be, and they saw a way to apply their talents to this end. Mildred Bulpitt learned about these colleges while taking a graduate course from Marty Martorana. "It was one of the most fascinating things I had heard of. In Connecticut we didn't have community colleges in those days. Washington State already had some junior colleges, and we thought junior colleges sounded nice, so when I got my master's in 1950, that's where I applied [to teach]."[13]

While pursuing her master's degree, Carolyn Desjardins learned from a friend that Phoenix College needed a dean of women. After a year in that position, "she had fallen in love with community colleges." Suanne Roueche "didn't feel right" as a high school teacher and began talking with friends about the newly created El Centro College. Once employed there, she found the students "to be more engaging" and the challenge to help them succeed "compelling."[14]

The women of the tribal colleges explicitly copied from the community college movement; they saw it as the form of higher education that was centered on meeting the needs of the students and local community.

Similarly, Wilhelmina Delco saw the promise of community colleges for the black population while on the local school board. "Community colleges represented a viable alternative [to public universities and private colleges]: they were closer, cheaper, and more flexible. They seemed to be an avenue for hope."[15] It was this revelation that compelled her to throw her support behind the proposed ballot measure to establish a community college district in Austin.

After failing to find a sense of collegiality in the university setting, Janet Lieberman moved into community college education and never looked back. "The challenge is what appealed to me," she recalls. "Status and money it was not." Through her varied innovative programs to assist the largely immigrant, first-generation college-going population of LaGuardia Community College, Janet came to believe in the importance of the "socialization factor" that community colleges had to offer this population: 'the extra-academic,' the 'richness of life-what's-out-there,' and 'setting your sights higher.'"[16]

Despite the fact that others recognize the mark these women made, many of the subjects demurred when asked what was their contribution to the community college movement.

Pat Cross replied to the question, "Would you say you helped shape America's community colleges?" by saying, "I don't think so. I think community colleges were well on their way. I think community colleges were to a large measure shaped locally."[17]

In response to the question, "What contributions have you made to community colleges?" Connie Sutton-Odems replied, "I'm a caring person. Honestly . . . I can't come up with anything . . . I'm blind; I don't see it."[18] When asked if she thought she made a unique contribution to the field of developmental education, Suanne Roueche said, "No, I made a consistent contribution but not a unique one."[19]

This tendency is not unlike what Heilbrun asserted:

> Indeed, to a striking degree they [famous women who wrote autobiographies] fail directly to emphasize their *own* importance. . . . These women accept full blame for any failures in their lives, but shrink from claiming that they either sought the responsibilities they ultimately bore or were in any way ambitious.[20]

Their humility notwithstanding, five of these women—Margaret Mosal, Pat Cross, Wilhelmina Delco, Carolyn Desjardins, and Suanne Roueche— received the National Leadership Award from the American Association of Community Colleges. This distinguished award is presented to individuals "whose accomplishments and professional contributions to the community college field have been outstanding."[21]

Finally, it is important to view these women's careers against the backdrop of the era in which they made their contributions. Even into the 1980s, many women found themselves in the mold of being subservient, the "good girl" everyone counted on to get the job done without drawing attention to herself. The subjects of this book possessed something within them—an inner drive, a passion, a clear focus—that allowed them to rise above these confining expectations.

Through their work, they encouraged others, deliberately or inadvertently, to see the possibilities for themselves. All were extremely bright, even visionary, but at the same time were firmly grounded in reality. Future generations—men and women alike—can be grateful for their dedication to improving teaching, learning, leadership, programs, and responsiveness in America's community colleges.

Appendix A

Methodology: Selecting the Subjects and Research Approach

How does one go about selecting a list of "best of" something? In this case, the standard approaches seemed inadequate or impossible. Tallying citations or references in the literature would be dependent upon reliable documentation about primary players during this era. However, much of the written record focuses, naturally enough, on community colleges themselves, rather than on the personalities behind the movement's development. Conducting a poll to elicit names of women leaders and innovators raised the question of how to select those to be polled.

Truly, the optimal method available was to speak extensively with those still living who were active nationally or regionally or in their particular field; to establish a set of criteria; and then to determine who best matched them based upon the interviews and literature review.

The initial research phase involved combining my knowledge of the community college movement, conducting telephone and in-person interviews with more than fifty people who were active in the growth years of the movement, and analyzing available publications and documents. Through these methods, the names arose repeatedly of some thirty women who were widely known and respected in community colleges.

Narrowing the field to allow in-depth research on a smaller number of subjects, I chose the following criteria to select the final subjects: They had to be women a) who made a definitive (singular) contribution of national import; b) who had made their contribution by 1990, as it became clear that by the early 1990s, the number of prominent women in the field began to proliferate—especially in the administrative ranks; c) whose names and contributions were recognized by at least several interviewees; and d) who were retired or dead.[1]

Regrettably, eliminating women who were still actively employed when I began the research (2003) for this book leaves out prominent leaders such as Judith Eaton, an early president and vocal advocate for the transfer function; Alison Bernstein, who helped fund hundreds of innovative projects through the Fund for the Improvement of Postsecondary Education and the Ford Foundation; Constance Carroll, a long-serving African American female president and a national leader in the humanities; Joyce Tsunoda, the first Asian American woman to head a multicampus community college system; and Piedad Robertson, a recognized early leader in international education and innovative programming.

A number of other women received multiple mentions from interviewees; however, their contributions occurred largely after 1990. These included college presidents or chancellors Jacquelyn M. Belcher, Eileen T. Farley, Pamila R. Fisher, Juliet V. Garcia, Jerry Sue Thornton, and Gwen Stephenson, and policy analyst and consultant Kay McClenney.

Some women did not make the final list because of a paucity of information about them. Marjorie K. Blaha, an early and nationally active California community college president, and Alice Thurston, a leader in student personnel, are two such examples. Others, such as Dorothy Donohoe, chairperson of the commission on the California Master Plan for Higher Education, had a tremendous impact on the evolution of community colleges but only within a single state. Many other women who instigated the formation of community college districts in their city were suggested for inclusion but did not meet the criterion of "national import."

Another subject I had hoped to include, Mina P. Shaughnessy, is legendary in the East for her pioneering work while at City University in New York in addressing the needs of students lacking basic writing skills. But after reading the definitive and compelling biography on Mina and her contributions,[2] I instead commend interested readers to that source.

In the end, the subjects selected are not as representative ethnically or geographically as one would hope. A poll taken today of "women of influence in community colleges" would no doubt include more women of color and women from the midwestern states. It certainly would include more presidents and chancellors.

Interestingly, most of the subjects selected spent the majority of their careers outside community colleges rather than within. Richard Alfred offered an insight in this regard: "When you're working at a college, it's your primary focus. Unless you are writing, you have limited influence outside your institution."[3] Interviewees generally agreed that, although many women were doing important things within community colleges, they spent little time trying to make a name for themselves outside their colleges. And, during most of this period, few women served as college CEOs.

Although I sought the opinions of many in choosing the final subjects, in the end the decisions were solely mine.[4] Ultimately, I had to discern those who I believed best met the criteria. The women selected represent an array of contributions—student services, research, policy, advocacy, curriculum, leadership development. Those selected, and their singular contribution to America's community college, are:

- Mildred Bulpitt and Carolyn Desjardins: Developing Women Leaders
- K. Patricia Cross: Influential Writer and Speaker
- Wilhelmina Delco: Giving Voice to Education's Underrepresented
- Dorothy Knoell: Respected Researcher
- Janet Lieberman: Serving At-Risk Youth
- Marie Y. Martin: Federal Advocate
- Jane Matson: Mentor for Student-Development Personnel
- Mildred Montag: Innovator in Nursing Education
- Margaret Mosal: Champion for High-Achieving Students
- Connie Sutton-Odems: National Association Leadership
- Suanne Roueche: Celebrating Teaching Excellence
- Women of the Tribal Colleges: Extending the Model

Once the subjects were selected, I traveled to visit most of those who were still living and interviewed them in person.[5] Interviews were tape-recorded and transcribed. Further insights were gained from telephone or in-person interviews with fifty-plus people "in positions to know." Included in that list are all of those who had headed the American Association for Community Colleges between 1957 and 2004,[6] nationally prominent college presidents/chancellors during this period,[7] university professors who specialized in community colleges,[8] and other directors or former leaders of national organizations.[9]

All available published works by the subjects were studied; books on community colleges were analyzed for references to their contributions.

Internet searches were conducted on each subject. These findings were used to corroborate or augment interview findings. K. Patricia Cross, for instance, has written extensively, is well-known so that everyone had something to say about her, and was willing to grant a lengthy personal interview.

The written record for other of these women is almost nonexistent. Margaret Mosal's life story came almost entirely from Rod Risley, who followed her as executive director of Phi Theta Kappa. Serious detective work was needed to learn about Marie Y. Martin's background. Sources for her story were as diverse as the University of California, Berkeley, alumni office; the student newspaper archives at Los Angeles Pierce College; and former colleagues who had long left the community college arena. Even the American Association of Community College Trustees—which has an award named in her honor—had little information on her background.

Through careful synthesis of the data collected on each woman, a picture emerges of her background, influences, career path, and contributions. Because I became so familiar with these women and their life stories during the course of my research, I refer to them by first name in the profiles. On the other hand, those persons speaking about the women are referred to by their full names.

After each profile was drafted, I shared it with the subject herself or, if she was deceased, with someone acknowledged to have been close to her professionally. The subjects reviewed the draft of their profile and edited for factual accuracy.

Ultimately, I hope these profiles paint a picture of how women rose to prominence in a time when gender barriers existed, when little was expected of them professionally, and when choosing community college education as the focus of their work meant going against the established academic grain. I found as I listened to their stories that, taken together, they amplify the history of community colleges during this period. In the course of their lives, these women made their mark on the evolving—and, at the time, unique—educational innovation known as the community college.

Appendix B

Acronyms

AAJC (American Association of Junior Colleges). Founded in 1925 and intended to function as an accrediting body for junior colleges, it became the forum for promoting and enhancing the mission of two-year colleges. In 1972, changed its name to

AACJC (American Association of Community and Junior Colleges). In 1992, changed its name to

AACC (American Association of Community Colleges).

ACCT (Association of Community College Trustees). Founded in 1972, this organization of governing boards represents the interests of elected and appointed trustees of community, technical, and junior colleges.

AAWCJC (American Association for Women in Community and Junior Colleges). Founded in 1973 by twenty-two women from Arizona, California, Oregon, and Washington. Accepted by the AACJC as a council member in 1974. Later changed its name to American Association for Women in Community Colleges.

AIHEC (American Indian Higher Education Consortium). Founded in 1973 to work for passage and funding of federal legislation to support the burgeoning tribal college movement.

ETS (Educational Testing Service). Founded in 1947 when the American Council on Education, the Carnegie Foundation for the Advancement of

Teaching, and the College Entrance Examination Board contributed their testing programs, a portion of their assets, and key employees to form ETS.

FISPE (Fund for the Improvement of Postsecondary Education). Established under the 1972 Higher Education to provide federal grants to support innovative educational reform projects that could serve as national models for the improvement of postsecondary education.

NILD (National Institute for Leadership Development). An outgrowth of the FIPSE-funded Leaders for the '80s project and housed at Phoenix College, NILD (now called the Leaders Institute) offers professional-development programs for women in community colleges.

NDEA (National Defense Education Act). Federal legislation passed in 1958 as a means to stimulate the advancement of education in science, mathematics, and modern foreign languages. It has also provided aid in other areas, including technical education, area studies, geography, English as a second language, counseling and guidance, school libraries and librarianship, and educational media centers.

Appendix C
Interviews with Author

Alfred, Richard. (2003, July 17). Telephone interview.

Bassett, Max. (2003, June 30). Telephone interview.

Bell, Priscilla. (2003, January 29). Telephone interview.

Bernstein, Alison. (2003, June 27). Personal interview.

Berringer, Bob. (2004, February 13). Telephone interview.

Berry, David. (2004, June 19). Telephone interview.

Bia, Johnson. (2005, July 19). Personal interview.

Boggs, George. (2004, February 12). Telephone interview.

Bratone, Barbara. (2005, September 21). Telephone interview.

Bulpitt, Mildred. (2003, September 29). Telephone interview.

Callan, Patrick. (2003, July 8). Telephone interview.

Carroll, Constance. (2005, December 21). Telephone interview.

Coracides, Carmen. (2003, October 2). Telephone interview.

Crawford, Michael. (2003, July 1). Telephone interview.

Cross, K. Patricia. (2003, July 8). Personal interview.

Davis, Carol. (2005, September 9). Telephone interview.

Davitt, John. (2003, August 20). Telephone interview.

Delco, Wilhelmina. (2003, June 9). Personal interview.

de los Santos, Alfredo. (2004, May 30). Telephone interview.

Desjardins, Sandra. (2003, October 2). Telephone interview.

Duncan, Mary Ellen. (2004, March 26). Telephone interview.

Ellison, Nolen M. (2003, July 22). Telephone interview.

Elsner, Paul. (2003, September 26). Personal interview.

Ernst, Richard. (2003, July 15). Telephone interview.

Fryer, Thomas. (2003, August 15). Telephone interview.

Garrison, Don. (2003, June 30). Telephone interview.

Gleazer, Edmund J., Jr. (2003, May 21). Personal interview. (2004, March 16). Telephone interview.

Hockaday, Johnas F. (2003, July 1). Telephone interview.

Hogan, Margaret. (2004, May 28). Telephone interview.

Hungar, Julie. (2003, May 9). Telephone interview.

Kane, Marie Pepicello. (2003, June 12). Telephone interview.

King, Charles. (2004, February 16). Telephone interview.

Knoell, Dorothy. (2003, July 6). Personal interview.

Lieberman, Janet. (2003, October 2). Personal interview.

Lucas, Aubrey. (2003, July 29). Telephone interview.

Luskin, Bernard. (2003, July 2). Telephone interview.

McCabe, Robert. (2003, June 6). Telephone interview.

McLeod, Martha. (2005, September 9). Telephone interview.

McGrath, Dennis. (2003, May 8). Telephone interview.

McHargue, Mike. (2004, August 24). Telephone interview.

Meardy, William. (2003, July 3). Telephone interview.

Mensel, Frank. (2003, October 30). Telephone interview.

Montag, Mildred. (2003, July 30). Telephone interview.

Nesbitt, Martha. (2003, May 30). Telephone interview.

O'Banion, Terry. (2003, June 5). Telephone interview.

Parnell, Dale. (2003, May 22). Telephone interview.

Phelps, Don. (2003, June 10). Telephone interview.

Pierce, David R. (2003, July 2). Telephone interview.

Popeck, Jack. (2004, February 9). Telephone interview.

Quigley, Martin S. (2003, June 12). Telephone interview.

Richardson, Richard C. (2003, June 6). Telephone interview.

Risley, Rod. (2003, May 27). Telephone interview. (2004, March 12). Telephone interview.

Rooney, Mike. (2003, July 16). Telephone interview.

Roessel, Robert. (2005, August 22). Telephone interview.

Roessel, Ruth. (2005, August 22). Telephone interview.

Roueche, John. (2003, June 10). Personal interview.

Roueche, Suanne. (2003, June 9). Personal interview.

Rowden, Tom. (2016, April 21). Telephone interview.

Sandel, Robert. (2003, July 15). Telephone interview.

Scheirbeck, Helen M. (2006, February 14). Telephone interview.

Shanley, Jim. (2005, August 30). Telephone interview.

Simone, Beverly. (2003, August 18). Telephone interview.

Stein, Wayne. (2003, July 30). Telephone interview.

Sutton-Odems, Connie. (2003, July 28). Telephone interview.

Taylor, Ray. (2003, July 17). Telephone interview.

Vaughan, George. (2003, May 21). Telephone interview.

Watson, Norman. (2003, July 15). Telephone interview.

Wattenbarger, James. (2003, June 4). Telephone interview.

Wheelan, Belle. (2003, July 23). Telephone interview.

Wolin, Carrole. (2003, May 29). Telephone interview. (2003, June 4). Telephone interview.

Wyles, Barbara. (2004, February 9). Telephone interview.

Notes

PREFACE

1. According to Witt, A. A., Wattenbarger, J., Gollattscheck, J. F., & Suppiger, J. E. (1994). *America's community colleges: The first century*. Washington, DC: Community College Press, the following contributions are attributed to these men:

- William Rainey Harper—envisioned and implemented the notion of dividing the traditional four collegiate years into two equal parts, with the first to be known as the junior college.
- Leonard V. Koos—prolific author, researcher, and editor of the *Junior College Journal*.
- Doak Campbell—first executive secretary of the American Association of Junior Colleges (AAJC), 1923–1938.
- Walter Eells—first editor of the *Junior College Journal* and first full-time executive director of the AAJC, 1938–1945.
- George F. Zook—chaired the President's Commission on Higher Education ("Truman Report") and founded the AAJC.
- Jesse P. Bogue—executive secretary of the AAJC, 1946–1958, and a tireless evangelist for the junior college movement.
- Leland Medsker—leading post–World War II scholar on junior/community colleges.
- James Wattenbarger—architect of Florida's master plan for community colleges, which served as a model for other states in planning statewide community college systems.
- S. V. Martorana—as specialist for community and junior colleges in the U.S. Office of Education, he was instrumental in paving the way for federal support for two-year colleges.

- Edmund J. Gleazer, Jr.—as president of the American Association of Community and Junior Colleges (AACJC), 1957–1981, he led the association through its period of most rapid growth and promoted the community colleges as the catalyst for community renewal.
- B. Lamar Johnson—sponsored the first W. K. Kellogg Foundation-funded Junior College Leadership Program at the University of California at Los Angeles; authored the landmark book *Islands of Innovation*; and played a major role in creating the League for Innovation in Community Colleges.
- Terry O'Banion—executive director of the League for Innovation, 1983–1999.
- Dale Parnell—president of the American Association of Community Colleges (AACC), 1981–1991, he focused on heightening federal support and promoting partnerships between business and education.
- William H. Meardy—as executive director of the Association of Community College Trustees, he took it from a struggling organization to a thriving national association.
- Joseph Cosand—founding president of the St. Louis Junior College District, AAJC Board member, and U.S. deputy commissioner for higher education.

INTRODUCTION

1. Heilbrun, C. G. (1988). *Writing a woman's life*. New York: Ballantine Books, p. 31.

2. An exception is the comprehensive and highly readable *America's community colleges: The first century* by A. A. Witt et al.

PART I

1. The reader is directed to two excellent historical overviews. Witt, A. A., Wattenbarger, J., Gollattscheck, J. F., & Suppiger, J. E. (1994). *America's community colleges: The first century*. Washington, DC: Community College Press; and American Association of Community Colleges. (2001). *America's community colleges: A century of innovation*. Washington, DC: Community College. For a review of topics in more depth, see G. A. Baker III (Ed.), J. Dudziak & P. Tyler (Technical Eds.). (1994). *A handbook on the community college in America: Its history, mission, and management*. Westport, CT: Greenwood Press.

2. Witt et al. (1994), p. 48.

3. Witt et al. (1994), p. 97.

4. Witt et al. (1994), p. 109.

5. Witt et al. (1994), p. 120.

6. Long, W. R., & Sanders, C. (1947). Junior college directory, 1946. *Junior College Journal, 17* (5), 213–35, as cited in Witt et al., (1994), *America's community colleges: The first century.* Washington, DC: Community College Press, p. 121.

7. Bonos, A. B., Jr. (1948). Community colleges—the next major step in American education. *Junior College Journal, 18* (8), 425–33, as cited in Witt et al. (1994), *America's community colleges: The first century.* Washington, DC: Community College Press, p. 129.

8. Witt et al. (1994), p. 132.

9. Monroe, C. R. (1977). *Profile of the community college* (2nd ed.). San Francisco: Jossey-Bass, p. 4.

10. Where have all the private 2-year colleges gone? (2003, September 12). *Chronicle of Higher Education*, p. A23.

11. Carlsen, C. J., & Burdick, R. (1994). Linked in governance: The role of the president and the board of trustees in the community college. In G. A. Baker III (Ed.), J. Dudziak & P. Tyler, (Technical Eds.), *A handbook on the community college in America: Its history, mission, and management* (pp. 259–67). Westport, CT: Greenwood Press, p. 262.

12. Cohen, A. M., & Brawer, F. B. (1982). *The American community college.* San Francisco: Jossey-Bass, p. 29.

13. Vaughan, G. B., & Associates. (1983). *Issues for community college leaders in a new era.* San Francisco: Jossey-Bass, p. 45.

14. Carlsen & Burdick (1994), p. 262.

15. Margaret Mosal became national secretary of Phi Theta Kappa in 1935; Mildred Montag published her dissertation on nursing education in 1951.

16. Monroe (1977), p. 63, states that "even up to 1960, community colleges, as a group, had such a poor image in higher education circles that most senior institutions tended to ignore them."

17. Smith, K., Downs, B., & O'Connell, M. (2001). *Maternity leave and employment patterns: 1961–1995.* Current Population Reports, pp. 70–79. Washington, DC: U.S. Census Bureau.

18. "Female-to-Male Earnings Ratio and Median Earnings of Full-Time, Year-Round Workers 15 Years and Older by Sex: 1960 to 2010." U.S. Census Bureau, Current Population Survey, 1961 to 2011 Annual Social and Economic Supplements, Washington, DC. Retrieved April 26, 2016, from http://www.census.gov/prod/2011pubs/p60-239.pdf.

19. Gleazer, E. J., Jr. (1973, April 5). *The role of women in America's community colleges. Presentation at the meeting of the National Association of Women Deans and Counselors.* Self-published, p. 6.

20. Dziech, B. W. (1983). Changing status of women. In G. B. Vaughan & Associates, *Issues for community college leaders in a new era* (pp. 55–75). San Francisco: Jossey-Bass, p. 61.

21. Walton, K. D. (Ed.). (1996). *Against the tide: Career paths of women leaders in American and British higher education.* Bloomington, IN: Phi Delta Kappa Educational Foundation, p. 4.

22. DiCroce, D. M. (1995). Women and the community college presidency: Challenges and possibilities. In B. K. Townsend (Ed.), *New directions for community colleges, No. 89. Gender and power in the community college* (pp. 79–88). San Francisco: Jossey-Bass, p. 80, reports 136 female CEOs in 1992. Walton (1996, p. 4) puts the number at 106 in 1992 and 138 in 1995.

23. Also, between 1960 and 1972, the twelve universities around the country were awarded a total of $4.4 million by the W. K. Kellogg Foundation to run "Junior College Leadership Programs," to provide graduate education for the many high-level administrators who would be needed in these proliferating institutions. As a result of these programs, it was not unusual for a young man, groomed and mentored by his professors, to rise quickly into a presidential position shortly after completing his doctoral studies. It appears that few females benefited similarly.

24. Rossi, E. J. (1976). The women's movement: Have community colleges responded? *Community College Review, 3,* (3), p. 43.

25. Vaughan & Associates (1983), p. 1.

26. Monroe (1977), p. 15.

27. Gleazer (1973, April 5).

28. Deegan, W. L., Tillery, D., & Associates. (1985). *Renewing the American community college.* San Francisco: Jossey-Bass, p. 55.

29. Goodrich, A. L., Lezotte, L.W., & Welch, J. A. (1972/1973). Minorities in two-year colleges: A survey. *Junior College Journal, 43* (4), p. 28, as cited in Witt et al., *America's community colleges: The first century.* Washington, DC: Community College Press, p. 243.

30. Cross, K. P., & McCartan, A. M. (1984). *Adult learning: State policies and institutional practices.* ASHE-ERIC Higher Education Research Report No. 1. Washington, DC: Association for the Study of Higher Education, p. 6.

31. Cohen & Brawer (1982), p. 31.

32. Venn, G. *Man, Education, and work: post-secondary vocational and technical education.* Washington, DC: American Council on Education, 1964, pp. 88–89, as cited in Monroe (1977), *Profile of the community college* (2nd ed.). San Francisco: Jossey-Bass, p. 91.

33. Cohen & Brawer (1982), p. 196.

34. Monroe (1977), p. 34.

35. The Americans with Disabilities Act was not passed until 1990.

CHAPTER 1

1. Rod Risley, interview with author.
2. Risley, interview with author.
3. Aubrey K. Lucas, interview with author.
4. David Pierce, interview with author.
5. James Wattenbarger, interview with author.
6. In fact, in the years after Margaret's retirement, membership in PTK has grown significantly, increasing by 2005 to ninety-seven thousand students (from twenty-five thousand in 1987) elected to membership each year.
7. Pierce, interview with author.
8. Quote from George R. Boggs, AACC president, in Former college president honored for national leadership. (2005, February 1). *Community College Times*, p. 1.
9. Tom Rowden, interview with author.
10. Risley, interview with author.
11. Wyatt, G. (2014, October 10). Personal interview with Rowden, retrieved from https://youtu.be/1niAqAOo0MM.
12. Risley, interview with author.

CHAPTER 2

1. Adelphi University. (2004). Mildred Montag, first director of Adelphi University's school of nursing, passes away at age 95. Retrieved July 12, 2005, from http://events.adelphi.edu/news/2004/20040121.php.
2. Schorr, T. M., & Zimmerman, A. (1988). *Making choices, taking chances: Nurse leaders tell their stories*. St. Louis: C. V. Mosby, p. 275.
3. Schorr & Zimmerman (1988), p. 275.
4. Haase, P. T. (1990). *The origins and rise of associate degree nursing education*. Durham, NC: Duke University Press, p. 23.
5. All quotes from Mildred Montag, telephone interview with author (July 30, 2002) unless otherwise noted.
6. Adelphi University. (2004).
7. Montag, M. L., & Swenson, R. P. S. (1959). *Fundamentals in nursing care*. Philadelphia: W. B. Saunders, p. 18.
8. Haase (1990), p. 10.
9. James Wattenbarger, interview with author.
10. Haase (1990), p. 10.
11. Schorr & Zimmerman (1988), p. 277.

12. Montag, M. L. (1951). *The education of nursing technicians.* New York: G. P. Putnam & Sons, 1951. Reprinted 1971 by John Wiley & Sons, p. 89.

13. Montag (1951), p. 95.

14. Montag (1951), p. 96.

15. Montag (1951), p. 97.

16. Montag (1951), p. 95.

17. Montag (1951), p. 98.

18. Haase (1990), p. 24.

19. Schorr & Zimmerman (1988), p. 278.

20. Haase (1990), p. 13.

21. Haase reports that at this time, some eighty arrangements between junior colleges and hospital schools of nursing were in existence, but there were no freestanding junior college nursing programs, p. 23.

22. Later identified as Mrs. Nelson Rockefeller (Quigley, M. S., & Bailey, T. W. [2003]. *Community college movement in perspective: Teachers College responds to the Truman Commission.* Lanham, MD: Scarecrow Press, p. 20).

23. Haase (1990), p. 23. This latter distinction, in fact, has not come to pass, as most patient-care jobs are not distinguished by those with a two-year versus four-year degree.

24. Haase (1990), p. 36.

25. Haase (1990), p. 39.

26. Montag, M. L. (1959). Community college education for nursing: An experiment in technical education for nursing. Report of the Cooperative Research Project in Junior-Community College Education for Nursing. New York: McGraw-Hill, pp. 339–40.

27. Schorr & Zimmerman (1988), p. 278.

28. Montag & Swenson (1959), p. 21.

29. Haase (1990), p. 2.

30. Gleazer, E. J., Jr. (2003, March 31). *To be different is difficult.* Presentation to Community College Leadership Program. Self-published.

31. Barker, V. (1969). A profile of accredited associate degree nursing programs. *Junior College Journal, 39* (6), p. 94.

32. Quigley, M. S., & Bailey, T. W. (2003). *Community college movement in perspective: Teachers College responds to the Truman Commission.* Lanham, MD: Scarecrow Press, p. 25.

33. Haase (1990), p. 40.

34. Quigley & Bailey (2003), p. 25.

35. Haase (1990), p. 40.

36. One person from a baccalaureate program told Montag that she "had set nursing back twenty-five years" (interview with Montag). Debate about the desirability of two-year education for registered nurses continues to this day.

37. Included in the Nutting Collection is a "Statement to the New York State Joint Legislative Committee," from 1964, in which Dr. Montag carefully articulates the arguments favoring a change in regulation: that the CRP research date proved the necessary coursework and clinical experiences could be completed within two years, that the cost of nursing education is best placed on the whole of society rather than upon those persons "ill in hospitals"; that associate degree programs have "tapped a source of students not previously attracted to nursing programs or unable to enroll in one (e.g., older, male, married, with children)"; and that research showed that they were fully competent bedside nurses.

38. See Mary Adelaide Nutting Collection, Milbank Memorial Library, Teachers College, Columbia University.

39. Wattenbarger, interview with author.

40. Wattenbarger, interview with author.

41. For a complete history of the associate degree in nursing and Mildred Montag's role in its development, see Haase (1990).

42. National League for Nursing. (2016). Number of Basic RN Programs, Total and by Program Type: 2005 to 2014. *NLN DataViewTM*. Retrieved from http://www.nln.org/docs/default-source/newsroom/nursing-education-statistics/number-of-basic-rn-programs-total-and-by-program-type-2005-to-2014.pdf?sfvrsn=0.

43. National Council of State Boards of Nursing, Inc. (2015). Part II—2014 NCLEX Examination Statistics. *2014 Nurse Licensee Volume and NCLEX Examination Statistics*. Retrieved from https://www.ncsbn.org/15_2014_NCLEX-ExamStats_vol64.pdf.

44. Haase (1990), p. 170.

45. Sasmor, J. L. (2004). A tribute to Dr. Mildred Montag. *National Organization for Associate Degree Nursing newsletter, 21* (1), 3.

46. Wattenbarger, interview with author.

47. *Nursing Arts* (1953), *Nursing Care* (1959), *Nursing Concepts and Nursing Care* (1976).

48. Schorr & Zimmerman (1988), p. 279.

CHAPTER 3

1. Jack Popeck, interview with author.

2. Richard Alfred, interview with author.

3. Popeck, interview with author.

4. Connie Sutton-Odems, interview with author.

5. Alfred, interview with author.

6. Mike Rooney, interview with author.

7. John Davitt, interview with author.

8. Alfred, interview with author.
9. Terry O'Banion, interview with author.
10. Max Bassett, interview with author.
11. Paul Elsner, interview with author.
12. James Wattenbarger, interview with author.
13. Robert McCabe, interview with author.
14. Davitt, interview with author.
15. Popeck, interview with author.
16. Dorothy Knoell, interview with author.
17. Sutton-Odems, interview with author.
18. Richard C. Richardson, interview with author.
19. Rooney, interview with author.
20. Rooney, interview with author.
21. Suanne Roueche, interview with author.
22. Rooney, interview with author.
23. Alfred, interview with author.
24. Popeck, interview with author.
25. Richardson, interview with author.
26. Davitt, interview with author.
27. Davitt, interview with author.

CHAPTER 4

1. All quotes from Dorothy Knoell, interview with author (July 6, 2003).
2. Now the women's college of Rutgers, the State University of New Jersey.
3. Knoell, D. M., & Medsker, L. L. (1964). *Factors affecting performance of students from two- to four-year colleges and articulation between two- and four-year colleges.* Berkeley: Center for the Study of Higher Education, University of California.
4. Knoell, D. M., & Medsker, L. L. (1965). *From junior to senior college: A national study of the transfer student.* Washington, DC: American Council on Education.
5. Prager, C. (1994). The articulation function of the community college. In G. A. Baker III (Ed.), J. Dudziak & P. Tyler (Technical Eds.), *A handbook on the community college in America: Its history, mission, and management* (pp. 495–507). Westport, CT: Greenwood Press.
6. Witt, A. A., Wattenbarger, J., Gollattscheck, J. F., & Suppiger, J. E. (1994). *America's community colleges: The first century.* Washington, DC: Community College Press, p. 234.
7. Robert McCabe, interview with author.

8. K. Patricia Cross, interview with author.

9. Knoell, D. M. (1966). *Toward Educational Opportunity for All*. Albany: State University of New York. As cited in Pedersen, R. (1994). Challenges facing the urban community college: A literature review. In G. A. Baker III (Ed.), J. Dudziak & P. Tyler (Technical Eds.), *A handbook on the community college in America: Its history, mission, and management* (pp. 176–89). Westport, CT: Greenwood Press.

10. Pedersen, R. (1994). Challenges facing the urban community college: A literature review. In G. A. Baker III (Ed.), J. Dudziak & P. Tyler (Technical Eds.), *A handbook on the community college in America: Its history, mission, and management* (pp. 176–89). Westport, CT: Greenwood Press, p. 185.

11. Ibid., p. 186.

12. California Postsecondary Education Commission. (1976). *Through the open door: A study of patterns of enrollment and performance in California's community colleges*. Report 76-1. Sacramento: CPEC.

13. Knoell, D. M. (1982). The transfer function—One of many. In F. Kintzer (Ed.), *New directions for community colleges: No. 39. Improving articulation and transfer relationships* (pp. 5–17). San Francisco: Jossey-Bass; and Knoell, D. M. (1983). Serving today's diverse students. In G. B. Vaughan & Associates, *Issues for community college leaders in a new era* (pp. 21–38). San Francisco: Jossey-Bass.

14. Alfredo de los Santos, interview with author.

15. Patrick M. Callan, interview with author.

16. Paul Elsner, interview with author.

17. Dick Alfred, interview with author.

18. Mike Rooney, interview with author.

19. Alison Bernstein, interview with author.

20. Callan, interview with author.

21. John Roueche, interview with author.

22. Elsner, interview with author.

23. Bernard Luskin, interview with author.

24. David Pierce, interview with author.

25. Knoell, D. M. (1990). *Transfer, articulation and collaboration twenty-five years later*. Washington, DC: American Association of Community and Junior Colleges.

CHAPTER 5

1. Title III Part A of the Higher Education Act includes the Strengthening Institutions Program, which assists eligible institutions of higher education to become self-sufficient by providing funds to improve and strengthen their academic quality, and institutional, management, and fiscal stability. One-year planning grants and five-year development grants are awarded.

2. New president favorably impressed with Pierce. (1966, January 14). *L.A. Pierce College Roundup*, p. 1.

3. Interestingly, John Lombardi was named president of City College in 1955; one suspects his influence in moving her into these leadership positions.

4. New president favorably impressed with Pierce. (1966, January 14). *L.A. Pierce College Roundup*, p. 1.

5. This move was condemned by the Pierce Faculty Senate as "questionable" and politically motivated on the part of four members of the District Board of Trustees. In a newspaper editorial, student Byron Dare praised Dr. Martin as "a woman who not only hit home runs, but struck them out when they came up to bat." He reported that at a luncheon in honor of her "promotion," "I realized that she wasn't going to say anything to condemn her opponents, she is too much of a lady for anything like that." (Dare, B. [1970, September 24]. Martin moves mount. Board moves Martin. *L.A. Pierce College Roundup*, p. unknown).

6. Don Garrison, interview with author.

7. Ray Taylor, interview with author.

8. San Diego Community College later dropped out of the consortium.

9. Garrison, interview with author.

10. Michael Crawford, interview with author.

11. Charles King, interview with author.

12. Beverly Simone, interview with author.

13. Mary Ellen Duncan, interview with author.

14. Connie Sutton-Odems, interview with author.

15. Frank Mensel, interview with author.

16. Nolen Ellison, interview with author.

17. Crawford, interview with author.

18. Ellison, interview with author.

19. Crawford, interview with author.

20. Taylor, interview with author.

21. Ellison, interview with author.

22. Crawford, interview with author.

23. Duncan, interview with author.

24. Bob Berringer, interview with author.

25. Garrison, interview with author.

CHAPTER 6

1. Thomas Fryer, interview with author.

2. All quotes from K. Patricia Cross, interview with author (July 8, 2003).

3. Human Intelligence (2004, July 14). *Raymond B. Cattell* [bibliographic profile]. Retrieved January 6, 2006, from http://www.indiana.edu/~intell/rcattell.shtml.

4. Dean With a Smile: Patricia Cross [newspaper article] (1960, April 21). *New York Times.*

5. Cross, K. P. *Beyond the open door.* (1971). San Francisco: Jossey-Bass, p. 164.

6. Gardner, J. W. (1961). *Excellence: Can we be equal and excellent too?* New York: W. W. Norton & Company, as quoted in Cross, K. P. *Beyond the open door* (1971). San Francisco: Jossey-Bass, pp. 164–65.

7. Cross, K. P. (1968). The junior college student: A research description. Princeton, NJ: Educational Testing Service. As quoted in Gleazer, E. J., Jr. (2003, March 31). To be different is difficult. Presentation to Community College Leadership Program. Self-published, p. 6.

8. Vaughan, G. B., & Ross, R. A. (1980). Works having a significant impact on the development of the community college in the United States. *Community/Junior College Research Quarterly*, (5), p. 12.

9. David R. Pierce, interview with author.

10. George Boggs, interview with author.

11. Nolen Ellison, interview with author.

12. Richard Ernst, interview with author.

13. Cross, K. P. (1976). *Accent on learning: Improving instruction and shaping the curriculum.* San Francisco: Jossey-Bass; Cross, K. P. (1981). *Adults as learners.* San Francisco: Jossey-Bass. Cross notes with amusement that, with publication of each new book, Jossey-Bass increased the prominence of her name on the book cover: from 16-point font (*Open Door*), to 22-point (*Accent*), to 56-point for *Adults as Learners.*

14. Cross, K. P. (1986). *Accent on learning.* San Francisco: Jossey-Bass, p. xi.

15. Both *Beyond the Open Door* and *Accent on Learning* were named as two of the thirteen works that "have had major influence on the field of developmental education," as selected by the editors of the *Journal of Developmental Education, 9* (1), (1985), p. 21. Readers were urged to read or reread these works, as they "influence the principles and practices used daily by developmental educators." *Accent on Learning* was also chosen as one of the ten "Best on Learning: A Bibliography of Essential Sources for Instructors" by Maryellen Gleason (1985) in *College Teaching, 33* (1), p. 9.

16. Dale Parnell, interview with author.

17. James Wattenbarger, interview with author.

18. Cross, K. P., & Angelo, T. A. (1988). *Classroom assessment techniques: A handbook for faculty.* Ann Arbor: National Center for Research to Improve Postsecondary Teaching and Learning, University of Michigan.

19. Beverly Simone, interview with author.

20. Suanne Roueche, interview with author.

21. Janet Lieberman, interview with author.

22. Lee Shulman, as quoted in "A Dedication to Education," *Illinois State for Alumni* (2001) 2, (4), p. 10.

23. Robert McCabe, interview with author.

CHAPTER 7

The author is deeply indebted to Harold S. Wechsler for his contributions to this profile. In his book *Access to Success in the Urban High School* (2001). New York: Teachers College Press, Wechsler chronicles the genesis, initiation, and replication of the middle-college movement in detail. The present account includes direct citations from that work.

1. All quotes from Janet Lieberman from interview with author (October 2, 2003).

2. Fiorello H. LaGuardia Community College, *Objectives and Programs*, p. 3, as quoted in *Middle College Proposal*, 1973, p. 5.

3. In 1969, officials at the City University of New York announced they would find places for all New York City high school graduates somewhere in the university, beginning in fall 1970. Although this intent had been official policy ("open admissions") for several years, the original 1975 target implementation date was accelerated in response to intense racial tensions surrounding college access. But the lack of adequate student preparation at the high school level, with many students dropping out by age sixteen, threatened the promise of guaranteed admission.

4. *Summary of activity on middle college proposal.* (1972). Middle College Archives, Middle College evaluation file.

5. Dunham, E. A. (1969). *Colleges of the forgotten Americans: A profile of state colleges and regional universities*. New York: McGraw-Hill.

6. Gehring, J. (2001, May 14). High school, with a college twist. *Education Week*, p. 2.

7. These outcomes data have varied over the years but typically exceed the average citywide rates in New York.

8. Alfredo de los Santos, interview with author.

9. Paul Elsner, interview with author.

10. Prager, C. (1994). The articulation function of the community college. In G. A. Baker III (Ed.), J. Dudziak & P. Tyler (Technical Eds.), *A handbook on the*

community college in America: Its history, mission, and management (pp. 495–507). Westport, CT: Greenwood Press, p. 502.

11. These include Middle College, International High School, Transfer Opportunities Program, and Exploring Transfer (with Vassar College).

12. In fact, Janet had gone by subway to her office on September 11, 2001. With public transportation shut down after the Twin Towers fell, she had to walk home the three miles to her Manhattan apartment via the Queensboro Bridge—at eighty years of age.

CHAPTER 8

1. All quotes from Connie Sutton-Odems are from interview with author (July 28, 2003).

2. Now Hampton University.

3. Founded in 1947, NTL Institute, headquartered in Alexandria, Virginia, is a not-for-profit educational company of members and staff whose purpose is to advance the field of applied behavioral sciences and to develop change agents for effective leadership for organizations of all kinds.

4. See profile on Marie Martin for additional details on the ACCTion Consortium.

5. Witt, A. A., Wattenbarger, J., Gollattscheck, J. F., & Suppiger, J. E. (1994). *America's community colleges: The first century.* Washington, DC: Community College Press, p. 267.

6. Vaughan, G. B., & Associates. (1983). *Issues for community college leaders in a new era.* San Francisco: Jossey-Bass, p. 10.

7. Dale Parnell, interview with author.

8. According to Witt et al. (1994), p. 206, "AACJC became the national center for research and studies related to community and junior colleges, and the host of annual meetings featuring the most respected and recognized leaders in the movement."

9. Richard Alfred, interview with author.

10. Richard Ernst, interview with author.

11. Donald Phelps, interview with author.

12. Johnas F. Hockaday, interview with author.

13. Nolen Ellison, interview with author.

14. Alfredo de los Santos, interview with author.

15. Ellison, interview with author.

16. Wilhelmina Delco, interview with author.

17. Belle Wheelan, interview with author.

18. Ellison, interview with author.

19. Edmund J. Gleazer Jr., interview with author.

20. Phelps, interview with author.

21. John Roueche, interview with author.

22. Ellison, interview with author.

CHAPTER 9

1. "They were directly responsible for changing the face of leadership in community colleges"; Margaret Hogan, interview with author. "NILD was the most important structure in the history of the community college movement to help women move up into leadership positions"; Terry O'Banion, League for Innovation, interview with author. "[Carolyn Desjardins] changed the community colleges of America"; Constance Carroll (San Diego Mesa College), *The Mesa Legend News*, August 25, 1997. "The increase of women [community college] presidents in the United States can be directly attributed to Desjardins"; Myrna Harrison (Phoenix College), *The Mesa Legend News*, August 25, 1997.

2. All quotes from Mildred Bulpitt, interview with author (September 29, 2003).

3. See part III for description of how Mildred was chosen for this job.

4. Paul Elsner, interview with author.

5. From 1975 to 1985, Mildred was also active as a consultant-evaluator for the North Central Association of Schools and Colleges and for five years served as one of its commissioners.

6. Later renamed the American Association of Women in Community Colleges, AAWCC, in 1993.

7. Edmund J. Gleazer Jr., interview with author.

8. Beverly Simone, interview with author.

9. Chronology based upon October 25, 1983, memorandum on the History of the FIPSE Project to the executive board of AACJC from Mildred Bulpitt.

10. Simone, interview with author.

11. Simone, interview with author.

12. O'Banion, interview with author.

13. O'Banion, interview with author.

14. Johnas F. Hockaday, interview with author.

15. Sandra Desjardins, interview with author.

16. Desjardins, interview with author.

17. Bourque, M., & Cvancara, K. J. (1995, January 24). Leaders all: Co-hen, Desjardins, McCabe are AACC leadership winners. *Community College Times*, p. 1.

18. Mildred Bulpitt, interview with author.

19. Hogan, interview with author.

20. Elsner, interview with author.

21. James Wattenbarger, interview with author.

22. Robert McCabe, interview with author.

23. E-mail correspondence with author (December 21, 2005).

24. Simone, interview with author.

25. Elsner, interview with author.

26. Martha Nesbitt, interview with author.

27. Desjardins, interview with author.

28. Carrole Wolin, interview with author.

29. Marie Pepicello, interview with author.

30. Wolin, interview with author.

31. Mike Rooney, interview with author.

32. Desjardins, C., with Huff, S. (2001). *The leading edge: Competencies for community college leadership in the new millennium.* League for Innovation in Community Colleges, Mission Viejo, CA.

33. Hogan, interview with author.

34. Elsner, interview with author.

35. DiCroce, D. M. (1995). Women and the community college presidency: Challenges and possibilities. In B. K. Townsend (Ed.), *New directions for community colleges, No. 89. Gender and power in the community college* (pp. 79–88). San Francisco: Jossey-Bass, p. 80.

36. Institute paves way for women to reach colleges' top rungs. (1996, March 15). *Houston Chronicle.*

37. Desjardins, interview with author.

CHAPTER 10

1. All quotes from Suanne Roueche are from interview with author (June 9, 2003).

2. Edmund J. Gleazer Jr., interview with author.

3. Robert McCabe, interview with author.

4. Johnas F. Hockaday, interview with author.

5. Milliron, M. D., & Wilson, C. (2004). No need to invent them: Community colleges and their place in the education landscape. *Change Magazine, 36* (6), pp. 52–57.

6. John Roueche, interview with author.

7. George Boggs, interview with author.

8. David Pierce, interview with author.

9. Robert Sandel, interview with author.

10. Sandel, interview with author.

11. Paul Elsner, interview with author.

12. John Roueche, interview with author.

13. Boggs, interview with author.

14. John Roueche, interview with author.

CHAPTER 11

1. All quotes from Wilhelmina Delco from interview with author (June 9, 2003).

2. For examples, see Flatau, S. K. (2000). *From my mother's hands: Remembrances and recipes from Texas women.* Plano, TX: Wordware Publishing; Pierce, P. J. (2002). *Let me tell you what I've learned: Texas wisewomen speak.* Austin: University of Texas Press; and The Wilhelmina Delco Collection of the John B. Coleman Library, Prairie View A&M University.

3. Now Huston-Tillitson University.

4. Delco, interview with author.

5. *The Honorable Wilhelmina Delco: Biography.* In The History Makers. (n.d.). Retrieved April 26, 2016, from http://www.thehistorymakers.com/biogra phy/honorable-wilhelmina-delco.

6. *Rodríguez v. San Antonio ISD.* Retrieved April 26, 2016, from Texas State Historical Association website, https://tshaonline.org/handbook/online/articles/ jrrht.

7. Instead, she served in the legislature for twenty years.

8. Retrieved March 15, 2005, from The Wilhelmina Delco Collection, http:// www.tamu.edu/pvamu/library/delco.htm.

9. John Roueche, interview with author.

10. Gleazer, E. A., Jr., Parnell, D., & Pierce, D. Years in the life: Former presidents reflect on the American Association of Community Colleges. *Community College Journal, 71* (5), p. 18.

11. Witt, A. A., Wattenbarger, J., Gollattscheck, J. F., & Suppiger, J. E. (1994). *America's community colleges: The first century.* Washington, DC: Community College Press, p. 269.

12. Connie Sutton-Odems, interview with author.

13. Nolen Ellison, interview with author.

14. Sutton-Odems, interview with author.

15. Witt et al. (1994), p. 269.

16. Beverly Simone, interview with author.

17. Robert Sandel, interview with author.

18. Suanne Roueche, interview with author.

19. Terry O'Banion, interview with author.

20. Belle Wheelan, interview with author.

21. Donald Phelps, interview with author.

22. Ellison, interview with author.

23. Dale Parnell, interview with author.

24. Paul Elsner, interview with author.

25. David Pierce, interview with author.

26. K. Patricia Cross, interview with author.

27. James Wattenbarger, interview with author.

CHAPTER 12

1. Ambler, M. (2002). Today's educators creating the leaders of tomorrow. *Tribal College Journal, 13* (4), 8.

2. Stein, W. J. (1990). The funding of tribally controlled colleges. *Journal of American Indian Education, 30* (1).

3. Roessel, R. A., Jr. (1972). A light in the night. *Journal of American Indian Education, 11* (3), 28.

4. Annual Report of the Lilly Endowment. (1999). Indianapolis, IN.

5. Roessel (1972), p. 28.

6. Ambler, M. (2002). Thirty years strong. *Tribal College Journal, 14* (2), 6.

7. Navajo Community College was renamed Diné College in 1997.

8. AIHEC honors tribal college founders. *Tribal College Journal, 12* (1), 8–9.

9. Boyer, P. (1997). *Native American colleges: Progress and prospects.* Princeton, NJ: The Carnegie Foundation for the Advancement of Teaching, p. 25.

10. Davis, T. (2001). Devotion to the people: The legacy of Helen Scheirbeck. *Tribal College Journal, 12* (4), 34.

11. Wayne Stein, interview with author.

12. D-Q University, Standing Rock Community College, Navajo Community College, Turtle Mountain Community College, Sinte Gleska College, and Oglala Sioux Community College were the six founders of AIHEC.

13. Stein (1990).

14. Davis (2001), p. 32.

15. All quotes from Helen Maynor Scheirbeck from interview with author (February 14, 2006).

16. Navajo Community College, rather than standing in the way of those who followed its lead, served as the sponsoring college for the first Title III grant supporting AIHEC. See Stein, W. J. (1992). *Tribally controlled colleges: Making good medicine.* New York: Peter Lang, p. 111.

17. Pease-Pretty on Top, J. (2003). Events leading to the passage of the tribally controlled community-college act of 1978. *Journal of American Indian Education, 42* (1), 11.

18. The first congressional action on tribal colleges was in early 1975, when it passed the Indian Self-Determination Act and included a provision that the Bureau of Indian Affairs study the need for federal funding of tribal colleges. Tribal college presidents and AIHEC leaders traveled frequently to Washington for the next several years to lobby for recognition and support. Finally in 1978, Congress passed, and President Jimmy Carter signed, P.L. 95-471, the Tribally Controlled Community College Assistance Act. Delayed by feasibility studies and rulemaking, tribal colleges did not receive appropriations under the act until 1980. See Pease-Pretty on Top. (2003).

19. Jim Shanley, interview with author.

20. Carol Davis, interview with author.

21. Roger Ironcloud, as quoted in Davis, T. (2001). Devotion to the people: The legacy of Helen Scheirbeck. *Tribal College Journal, 12* (4), 39.

22. Janine Pease is also known as Janine Pease-Pretty on Top and Janine Pease-Windy Boy.

23. Shanley, interview with author.

24. Martha McLeod, interview with author.

25. Stein, interview with author. Stein points out that, in American Indian circles, Pease is often best known for being the lead plaintiff in a historic voting-rights suit in the 1980s, *Windy Boy v. Big Horn County et al.* The federal district court ruled for the plaintiffs, ordering the redesign of school board and county commissioner districts to provide for Indian majority districts based upon population.

26. Helen Maynor Scheirbeck, interview with author.

27. We just can't fail. (1991). *Tribal College Journal, 2* (4), 17.

28. Barbara Bratone, interview with author.

29. Shanley, interview with author.

30. Shanley, interview with author.

31. Janine Pease, a founding board member, also played an important role in the early years of the American Indian College Fund, according to Jim Shanley.

32. Shanley, interview with author.

33. American Indian Higher Education Consortium. (2015). [Graph illustration October 2015]. *Tribal colleges and universities enrollment by major group, Fall 2013.* Retrieved from http://www.aihec.org/who-we-serve/docs/TCU_En rollment_fall2013.pdf.

34. Stein, interview with author.

35. As quoted in Ambler, M. (1992). Women leaders in Indian education. *Tribal College Journal, 3* (4), 11. Crazy Bull was then vice president at Sinte Gleska University and later became president of Northwest Indian College.

36. Boyer (1997), p. 35.

37. Shanley, interview with author.

38. Delores Wilkinson, as quoted in Ambler, M. (1992). Women leaders in Indian education. *Tribal College Journal, 3* (4), 12.

PART III

1. Bateson, M. C. (1990). *Composing a life.* New York: Plume/Penguin, p. 5.

2. As four of the subjects (Carolyn Desjardins, Marie Martin, Jane Matson, and Margaret Mosal) were deceased at the time that interviews were conducted, certain background information was not available.

3. Ambler, M. (1992). Women leaders in Indian education. *Tribal College Journal, 3* (4), p. 11.

4. The three American Indian women (Roessel, Shierbeck, and Pease) were working within and for the cause of higher education for their people and did not mention issues of discrimination.

5. Connie Sutton-Odems, interview with author.

6. Mildred Bulpitt, interview with author.

7. Smith, K., Downs, B., & O'Connell, M. (2001). *Maternity leave and employment patterns: 1961–1995.* Current Population Reports P70-79. U.S. Census Bureau, Washington, D.C.

8. Heilbrun, C. G. (1988). *Writing a woman's life.* New York: Ballantine Books, p. 109.

9. Schorr, T. M., & Zimmerman, A. (1988). *Making choices, taking chances: Nurse leaders tell their stories.* St. Louis: C.V. Mosby, p. 276.

10. Haase, P. T. (1990). *The origins and rise of associate degree nursing education.* Durham, NC: Duke University Press, pp. 1–12.

11. K. Patricia Cross, interview with author.

12. Sutton-Odems, interview with author.

13. Bulpitt, interview with author.

14. Suanne Roueche, interview with author.

15. Wilhelmina Delco, interview with author.

16. Janet Lieberman, interview with author.

17. Cross, interview with author.

18. Sutton-Odems, interview with author.

19. Suanne Roueche, interview with author.

20. Heilbrun (1988), p. 23.

21. Only two other women have received the AACC National Leadership Award: Anne E. Mulder of Nova Southeastern University and Shirley B. Gordon for her work on Phi Theta Kappa's board of directors.

APPENDIX A

1. The exception is the profile on Women of the Tribal Colleges. When I came across "her-story," I was both immensely intrigued and at the same time taken aback at my lack of familiarity with what was basically a parallel track to the early community college movement and the role women played in it. This profile merely scratches the surface of the contributions of some remarkable women.

2. Maher, J. (1997). *Mina P. Shaughnessy: Her life and work.* Urbana, IL: National Council of Teachers of English.

3. Richard Alfred, interview with author.

4. Not all of the women selected received unanimous endorsement from interviewees. Some have national name recognition; others, more regional. A few are well-known, but their contributions were downplayed by some of the interviewees. Some were well-known by national leaders but not by people "in the field"; others were not well-known in general but were unequivocally recognized within a segment of community college education.

5. In-person interviews were conducted with Mildred Bulpitt, K. Patricia Cross, Wilhelmina Delco, Dorothy M. Knoell, Janet Lieberman, Connie Sutton-Odems, and Suanne D. Roueche. Phone interviews were conducted with Barbara Bratone, Mildred Montag, Ruth Roessel, and Helen Scheirbeck. Carolyn Desjardins, Marie Y. Martin, Jane Matson, Margaret Mosal were deceased at the time of writing.

6. Edmund G. Gleazer Jr., Dale Parnell, David Pierce, and George Boggs.

7. Nolen Ellison, Paul Elsner, Thomas Fryer, Don Garrison, Jeff Hockaday, Bernard Luskin, Robert McCabe, Donald G. Phelps, and Beverly Simone.

8. Richard L. Alfred, Richard C. Richardson, John E. Roueche, George B. Vaughan, and James Wattenbarger.

9. William Meardy, Terry O'Banion, Rod Risley, and Ray Taylor.

References

Adelphi University. (2004). Mildred Montag, first director of Adelphi University's school of nursing, passes away at age 95. Retrieved July 12, 2005, from http://events.adelphi.edu/news/2004/20040121.php.

Altback, P. G., & Berdahl, R. O. (Eds.). (1981). *Higher education in American society.* New York: Prometheus Books.

Ambler, M. (1992). Women leaders in Indian education. *Tribal College Journal, 3* (4), 10–15.

———. (2002). Today's educators creating the leaders of tomorrow. *Tribal College Journal, 13* (4), 8–9.

———. (2002). Thirty years strong. *Tribal College Journal, 14* (2), 6–9.

American Association of Community Colleges. (2001). *America's community colleges: A century of innovation.* Washington, DC: Community College Press.

Baker, G. A., III (Ed.), Dudziak, J., & Tyler, P. (Technical Eds.). (1994). *A handbook on the community college in America: Its history, mission, and management.* Westport, CT: Greenwood Press.

Barker, V. (1969). A profile of accredited associate degree nursing programs. *Junior College Journal, 39* (6).

Bateson, M. C. (1990). *Composing a life.* New York: Plume/Penguin.

Boyer, P. (1997). *Native American colleges: Progress and prospects.* Princeton, NJ: The Carnegie Foundation for the Advancement of Teaching.

California Postsecondary Education Commission. (1976). *Through the open door: A study of patterns of enrollment and performance in California's community colleges.* Report 76-1. Sacramento: CPEC.

Carlsen, C. J., & Burdick, R. (1994). Linked in governance: The role of the president and the board of trustees in the community college. In G. A. Baker III (Ed.), J. Dudziak & P. Tyler (Technical Eds.), *A handbook on the community college in America: Its history, mission, and management* (pp. 259–67). Westport, CT: Greenwood Press.

Clark, B. R. (1960). *The open door college: A case study.* New York: McGraw-Hill.

Cohen, A. M., & Brawer, F. B. (1982). *The American community college.* San Francisco: Jossey-Bass.

Cross, K. P. (1971). *Beyond the open door: New students to higher education.* San Francisco: Jossey-Bass.

———. (1976). *Accent on learning: Improving instruction and shaping the curriculum.* San Francisco: Jossey-Bass.

———. (1981). *Adults as learners.* San Francisco: Jossey-Bass.

Cross, K. P., & Angelo, T. A. (1988). *Classroom assessment techniques: A handbook for faculty.* Ann Arbor: National Center for Research to Improve Postsecondary Teaching and Learning, University of Michigan.

Cross, K. P., & McCartan, A. M. (1984). *Adult learning: State policies and institutional practices.* ASHE-ERIC Higher Education Research Report No. 1. Washington, DC: Association for the Study of Higher Education.

Davis, T. (2001). Devotion to the people: The legacy of Helen Scheirbeck. *Tribal College Journal, 12* (4), 32–35, 39.

Deegan, W. L., Tillery, D., & Associates. (1985). *Renewing the American community college.* San Francisco: Jossey-Bass.

DiCroce, D. M. (1995). Women and the community college presidency: Challenges and possibilities. In B. K. Townsend (Ed.), *New directions for community colleges, No. 89. Gender and power in the community college* (pp. 79–88). San Francisco: Jossey-Bass.

Dziech, B. W. (1983). Changing status of women. In G. B. Vaughan & Associates, *Issues for community college leaders in a new era* (pp. 55–75). San Francisco: Jossey-Bass.

Gleason, M. E. (1985). Best on learning: A bibliography of essential sources for instructors. *College Teaching, 33,* 1.

Gleazer, E. J., Jr. (April 5, 1973). *The role of women in America's community colleges.* Presentation at the meeting of the National Association of Women Deans and Counselors. Self-published.

———. Evolution of junior colleges into community colleges (1994). In G. A. Baker III (Ed.), J. Dudziak & P. Tyler (Technical Eds.), *A handbook on the community college in America: Its history, mission, and management* (pp. 17–27). Westport, CT: Greenwood Press.

———. (March 31, 2003). *To be different is difficult.* Presentation to Community College Leadership Program. Self-published.

Haase, P. T. (1990). *The origins and rise of associate degree nursing education.* Durham, NC: Duke University Press.

Heilbrun, C. G. (1988). *Writing a woman's life.* New York: Ballantine Books.

Knoell, D. M. (1966). *Toward educational opportunity for all.* Albany: State University of New York. As cited in Pedersen, R. (1994). Challenges facing the urban community college: A literature review. In G. A. Baker III (Ed.), J. Dudziak & P. Tyler (Technical Eds.), *A handbook on the community college in America: Its history, mission, and management* (pp. 176–189). Westport, CT: Greenwood Press.

———. (1982). The transfer function—One of many. In F. Kintzer (Ed.), *New directions for community colleges: No. 39. Improving articulation and transfer relationships* (pp. 5–17). San Francisco: Jossey-Bass.

———. (1983). Serving today's diverse students. In G. B. Vaughan & Associates, *Issues for community college leaders in a new era* (pp. 21–38). San Francisco: Jossey-Bass.

———. (1990). *Transfer, articulation and collaboration twenty-five years later.* Washington, DC: American Association of Community and Junior Colleges.

Knoell, D. M., & Medsker, L. L. (1965). *From junior to senior college: A national study of the transfer student.* Washington, DC: American Council on Education.

Milliron, M. D., & Wilson, C. (2004). No need to invent them: Community colleges and their place in the education landscape. *Change Magazine 36* (6).

Monroe, C. R. (1977). *Profile of the community college* (2nd ed.). San Francisco: Jossey-Bass.

Montag, M. L. (1951). *The education of nursing technicians.* New York: G. P. Putnam & Sons. Reprinted 1971 by John Wiley & Sons.

———. (1959). *Community college education for nursing: An experiment in technical education for nursing. Report of the Cooperative Research Project in Junior-Community College Education for Nursing.* New York: McGraw-Hill.

Montag, M. L., & Swenson, R. P. S. (1959). *Fundamentals in nursing care.* Philadelphia: W. B. Saunders.

Pease-Pretty on Top, J. (2003). Events leading to the passage of the tribally controlled community college act of 1978. *Journal of American Indian Education, 42*, (1), 6–21.

Pedersen, R. (1994). Challenges facing the urban community college: A literature review. In G. A. Baker III (Ed.), J. Dudziak & P. Tyler (Technical Eds.), *A handbook on the community college in America: Its history, mission, and management* (pp. 176–89). Westport, CT: Greenwood Press.

Prager, C. (1994). The articulation function of the community college. In G. A. Baker III (Ed.), J. Dudziak & P. Tyler (Technical Eds.), *A handbook on the community college in America: Its history, mission, and management* (pp. 495–507). Westport, CT: Greenwood Press.

President's Commission on Higher Education. (1947). *Higher education for American democracy.* New York: Harper & Brothers.

Quigley, M. S., & Bailey, T. W. (2003). *Community college movement in perspective: Teachers College responds to the Truman Commission.* Lanham, MD: Scarecrow Press.

Roessel, R. A., Jr. (1972). A light in the night. *Journal of American Indian Education, 11* (3), 26–29.

Rossi, E. J. (1976). The women's movement: Have community colleges responded? *Community College Review, 3* (3), 36–46.

Sasmor, J. L. (2004). A tribute to Dr. Mildred Montag. *National Organization for Associate Degree Nursing newsletter, 21* (1), 3.

Schorr, T. M., & Zimmerman, A. (1988). *Making choices, taking chances: Nurse leaders tell their stories.* St. Louis: C. V. Mosby.

Smith, K., Downs, B., & O'Connell, M. (2001). *Maternity leave and employment patterns: 1961–1995.* Current Population Reports P70-79. Washington, DC: U.S. Census Bureau.

Stein, W. J. The funding of tribally controlled colleges. (1990). *Journal of American Indian Education, 30* (1), 1–17.

———. (1992). *Tribally controlled colleges: Making good medicine.* New York: Peter Lang.

Touchton, J., & Ingram, D. *Women presidents in U.S. colleges and universities: A 1995 higher education update.* Washington, DC: American Council on Education. As cited in Walton (1996). *Against the tide: Career paths of women leaders in American and British higher education.* Bloomington, IN: Phi Delta Kappa Educational Foundation.

Vaughan, G. B., &Associates. (1983). *Issues for community college leaders in a new era.* San Francisco: Jossey-Bass.

Vaughan, G. B., & Ross, R. A. (1980). Works having a significant impact on the development of the community college in the United States. *Community/ Junior College Research Quarterly*, (5), 11–22.

Walton, K. D. (Ed.). (1996). *Against the tide: Career paths of women leaders in American and British higher education.* Bloomington, IN: Phi Delta Kappa Educational Foundation.

Wechsler, H. S. (2001). *Access to success in the urban high school: The middle college movement.* New York: Teachers College Press.

Witt, A. A., Wattenbarger, J., Gollattscheck, J. F., & Suppiger, J. E. (1994). *America's community colleges: The first century.* Washington, DC: Community College Press.

Index

175

About the Author

Anne-Marie McCartan recently completed forty years working at the national, state, and institutional levels of higher education. In 2016, she completed ten years as executive director of the Council of Colleges of Arts & Sciences. From 2004 to 2006 she was president of the Northwest Campus of Pima Community College in Tucson, Arizona. Previously, she was provost and dean of faculty at Richard Bland College, the junior college of the College of William & Mary. She served the Virginia Community Colleges System from 1993 to 1999 as its vice chancellor for academic and research services and one year as interim president of Rappahannock Community College.

A native of Washington State, McCartan received a bachelor's and master's degree from the University of Washington, and her doctorate in education from Harvard University. She resides in Richmond, Virginia, with her husband.

Made in the USA
Middletown, DE
23 April 2018